Psychic
Protection
For Beginners

About Richard Webster

Author of over forty titles published with Llewellyn, Richard Webster is one of New Zealand's most prolific writers. His best-selling books include *Spirit Guides & Angel Guardians, Creative Visualization for Beginners, Soul Mates, Is Your Pet Psychic?, Practical Guide to Past-Life Memories, Astral Travel for Beginners, Miracles,* and the four-book series on archangels: *Michael, Gabriel, Raphael,* and *Uriel.*

A noted psychic, Richard is a member of the National Guild of Hypnotherapists (USA), the Association of Professional Hypnotherapists and Parapsychologists (UK), the International Registry of Professional Hypnotherapists (Canada), and the Psychotherapy and Hypnotherapy Institute of New Zealand. When not touring, he resides in New Zealand with his wife and family.

Psychic Protection

For Beginners

Creating a Safe Haven for Home & Family

RICHARD WEBSTER

Llewellyn Publications
Woodbury, Minnesota

First Edition
First Printing, 2010

Editing by Laura Graves
Cover photo © Uwe Krejci/Digital Vision/PunchStock

Llewellyn is a registered trademark of Llewellyn Worldwide, Ltd.

Library of Congress Cataloging-in-Publication Data
Webster, Richard, 1946–
  Psychic protection for beginners: creating a safe haven for home & family / Richard Webster.—1st ed.
      p. cm.
  Includes bibliographical references (p.   ) and index.
  ISBN 978-0-7387-2060-9
  1. Self-defense—Psychic aspects. I. Title.
  BF1045.S46W43 2010
  133.8—dc22

                                        2010000728

Llewellyn Publications
A Division of Llewellyn Worldwide, Ltd.
2143 Wooddale Drive
Woodbury, MN 55125-2989
www.llewellyn.com

Printed in the United States of America

For Sandi Liss
and
Soul Journey

Also by Richard Webster

contents

introduction

While I was writing this book, a friend told me that he'd never needed psychic protection, as he led a "normal" life. This is a common misconception. I believe *everyone* needs psychic protection from time to time. I asked my friend a series of questions, and after answering them, he grudgingly admitted that maybe he could benefit from psychic protection after all. These are the questions I asked him:

Has anyone ever looked at you with "evil eyes"?

Do people regularly confide in you and tell you their problems?

Do you experience nightmares or unpleasant dreams?

Do you ever feel listless, apathetic, or unmotivated?

Do you suffer from headaches?

Do your everyday problems get you down?

Do you ever consume recreational drugs?

Do you ever feel exhausted after being in the company of someone else?

Have you ever felt intimidated by someone?

Do you ever feel out of control?

Do you experience days where nothing goes right?

Do you meditate or practice self-hypnosis?

Are you nervous or lacking in confidence?

Do you feel inferior to others?

Have you ever been bullied or tormented by others?

Are you a healer, therapist, or counselor?

Do you suffer from anxiety or experience panic attacks?

Do you see the glass as half-empty rather than half-full?

If you answered yes to any of these, you need psychic protection. You already protect yourself in a variety of ways. You live in a house that protects you from the elements. You invest your money, not only to earn interest, but also to keep it safe. You buy insurance to protect you from a variety of possible disasters. You probably avoid dangerous neighborhoods. These are all practical forms of protection. However, few people are aware of the need for psychic protection.

Sometimes our own minds can be our worst enemies. Here's an example. Several months ago, the fourteen-year-old daughter of friends of ours suffered a nervous breakdown. Her parents had no idea that she'd been receiving a constant stream of vicious, anonymous text messages. Because a cell phone is an essential item for most teenagers, the attacker was able to reach her easily at any time of the day or night. This meant the victim never felt safe, not even in her own bedroom. After her breakdown, the police and school became involved, and a former friend admitted to sending the texts. The attacker claimed it was simply a harmless prank, but her victim is still receiving help for the damage caused.

Unfortunately, at the time of the attack, our friends' daughter knew nothing about psychic protection. This incident shows that learning how to psychically protect yourself is just as important as any other form of protection. Thousands of years ago, our ancestors were aware of this.

The world was a dangerous place back then. In addition to the normal problems of everyday living, people believed invisible beings such as demons, evil spirits, and disembodied souls lived just beyond sight. It's not surprising people sought psychic protection to keep them safe from harm. Naturally, their main concern was for their safety and survival, and various ways were devised to protect them.

A house is a place people live in. A home is also a house that people live in, but it's much more than that. The word *home* makes us think of love, family, safety, security, and happiness. In earlier times, home was associated with the hearth, warmth, and the kitchen fire. Your home is a place for your physical body to live in, but it should also be a place where you can nurture your spirit and be free to express the real you. An old proverb says it all: "Home is where the heart is."

Safety should be one of the first things that come to mind when people think of *home*: homes are built to provide protection from the elements, predators, and other people. That's why we build walls around our homes and lock the doors.

Sadly, many homes are not safe. Children from dysfunctional families sometimes grow up and produce further generations of dysfunctional families.

Far too many people suffer verbal and physical abuse inside the one place where they should feel safe. Some people, especially mothers, are constantly giving to the rest of the family and have little or no time to nurture themselves. All of these people need some form of psychic protection to protect them from what's happening inside their home. Most people need psychic protection to protect them from potential danger outside the home as well.

Everyone can benefit from psychic protection. We all suffer from stresses, pressures, and antagonism at different times. Most people experience colds and minor illnesses from time to time. It would be hard to find someone who hasn't experienced the feelings of being physically, mentally, and emotionally drained every now and again. You need all the protection you can find at these times.

The thoughts, actions, and feelings of others can wear us down, too. For a while, I worked for a couple who were experiencing marital problems and constantly argued with each other. Almost every day I came home with a headache, as the environment was so stressful.

As most news on the television or radio is bad rather than good, it is usually a negative experience to watch or listen to the news. Newspapers focus on tragedies and disasters, as bad news sells more papers than good news. Because we are surrounded by negativity all the time, it is difficult to avoid picking up negativity from others. People who find it hard to say no to others are particularly prone to this. Some people are extremely sensitive to the moods and feelings of others, making them particularly susceptible to psychic attack.

Highly intuitive people are also affected this way. When I worked as a psychic reader, I had to be especially careful that my clients' attitudes, energies, and thoughts didn't drain me. Natural healers also need to clear themselves to avoid picking up the negative vibrations of their patients.

Even our own negative thoughts undermine us and consequently can be considered a form of self-inflicted psychic attack. Just recently, I worked with someone who does recreational drugs every now and again. He was trying to eliminate the substances from his life, as he had discovered they made him extremely open to psychic attack.

Geopathic stress created by electromagnetic radiation and underground water can affect the immune system, leaving a person open to physical illnesses as well as psychic attack. Sometimes it seems that we are all under some form of psychic attack.

Fortunately, we can protect ourselves, as well as our homes and loved ones, from intentional and unintentional invasions of these sorts. In fact, psychic protection could be considered an essential part of health and well-being. Psychic protection provides us with an invisible cocoon that surrounds and protects us from any form of attack, be it deliberate or unintentional. One lady told me that she felt surrounded by an extra layer of clear skin that kept her warm, secure, and safe, even while going through a difficult divorce. "Only positive energy could get through to me," she told me. "Everything else—all the stress and unpleasantness—was filtered away before it could reach me. I felt safe and protected all the time."

Psychic protection is more common than some people think. When astronaut Edward White went to the moon, he took with him a St. Christopher medal, a Star of David, and a gold cross.[1] To me, that makes perfect sense. If I went to the moon, I'd carry all of these and more.

The English author W. Somerset Maugham took the idea of protection very seriously. His father had obtained an amulet in Morocco showing a spiked arrow and a double cross. Somerset Maugham was fascinated with it and began using it as a personal symbol. It was inscribed on his personal possessions, engraved on the windows of his house, and printed on the covers of all his books. He believed implicitly that the amulet warded off evil, and he had evidence of this. One of his early novels, *The Hero*, was a total failure. On the cover of this book, the amulet had been accidentally printed upside down.

A good example of psychic protection occurs at Jewish weddings. At the end of the ceremony the bridegroom breaks an expensive glass. The noise created by breaking an expensive object is intended to divert the attention of any evil force away from the happy couple. The congregation shouts out *"Mazel tov!"* (good luck) as the glass is broken. Doing so provides protection: it ensures that no envious spirit can take away the couple's happiness.

Naturally, psychic protection doesn't mean you should break all your glasses or neglect to lock your house when you leave for any period of time. You shouldn't dispense with burglar alarms or smoke detectors either. Locking your car is a sensible thing to do, even if you have psychically protected it. You still need to pay attention to physical security by observing what is going on around you, avoiding bad neighborhoods, and being careful and mindful everywhere you go.

There is no single method of psychic protection that works well for everyone. Consequently, in this book you'll learn a variety of ways to protect yourself using many time-proven methods, including scents, crystals, gemstones, amulets, herbs, colors, candles, and meditation. Your aura is your most powerful defense against any form of psychic attack, and you'll learn how to strengthen your aura to gain additional protection. You'll discover how to ward off any deliberate psychic attack someone might direct at you. In addition, you'll also learn how to psychically protect your physical home and the special people in your life.

This book is not concerned with physical protection. Its sole purpose is to help you to psychically protect yourself and your loved ones, as well as your home and other possessions.

one

Psychic Protection

People have used psychic protection from well before the dawn of recorded history. Because the world was such a dangerous place full of invisible demons and evil spirits, people used every means at their disposal to protect their clan and food sources.

Amulets and talismans have been found in ancient burial sites, including the floor deposits of prehistoric cave dwellings.[1] Their owners probably wore them for protective purposes.

The ancient Egyptians had specific funerary amulets to help the deceased make their journey into the next world. Copies of the *Book of the Dead* were also placed inside the burial chamber, probably for some protective purpose.[2] The priests who carried out these burials also wore amulets and talismans for protection. High priests and priestesses were expert magicians who spent their lives attempting to placate evil spirits and attract good ones. Wearing amulets and charms made perfect sense, as they provided protection and attracted good luck. A funerary papyrus, known as the MacGregor Papyrus, includes illustrations of the seventy-five most popular amulets Egyptians used some three-and-a-half-thousand years ago. Depictions of 104 amulets can still be seen in a doorway on the roof of the Ptolemaic temple of the goddess Hathor at Dendera.

The ancient Carthaginians used smiling and scowling masks as protective amulets for both the living and the dead. The smiling masks were used to gain protection from the gods, while the scowling masks warded off evil spirits.[3]

However, once the concept of a god or gods became accepted, the religious establishment frowned on pagan amulets and charms because their deity was capable of providing all the protection anyone could need. Of course, the religions that developed were happy to allow amulets and charms *they* believed to have religious significance; they were above "superstition." It is hard to understand why the Christian

Church was so opposed to the use of amulets, as it was not anti-religious, and many amulets carried the names of the gods who provided the protection. St. John Chrysostom (c. 347–407) and other early Christian fathers condemned amulets, as they claimed they were connected with magic.[4] Even governments denounced amulets. The Roman emperor Caracalla (188–217) became concerned about the number of people wearing amulets and banned them. Heavy penalties were imposed on people who continued to wear them.[5]

As well as invisible spirits, psychic attack could come from other people. A curse is a form of psychic attack, and there have been numerous accounts of people wasting away and dying after receiving a curse.

The human eye has always been considered remarkable, as people can have different-colored irises and possess pupils that grow and contract in size. Thousands of years ago, people were aware of the little person they saw reflected in others' eyes. The Bible refers to this in "He kept him (Jacob) as the apple of his eye" (Deuteronomy 32:10), "Keep my commandments, and live; and my law as the apple of thine eye" (Proverbs 7:2), and "Keep me as the apple of the eye, hide me under the shadow of thy wings" (Psalms 17:8). Many people believed that the person seen in someone's eye could leave one person's eye and move into someone else's eye, where it could do harm.[6]

The eye is also used in several creation stories. Ptah, in Egyptian myth, was the creator of the universe. He produced all the other gods from his eyes.[7]

In another story, the sun god Ra became separated from his twin children, Shu and Tefnut. He sent his eye to search for them. While his eye was busy searching for his children, Ra inserted another eye in its place. His eye found the missing children and brought them back. Ra wept at the sight of them, and his tears created the human race. The eye was unhappy, though, to find another eye in his place. Ra placed this eye on his forehead, allowing it to rule the world. This eye became associated with the sun, and the other eye became associated with the moon.[8]

The Evil Eye

Because eyes are so expressive, they have always been considered capable of creating good or bad fortune. A look of love bestows good luck on the object of affection, while an angry glance has the potential to cause great harm. The evil eye is the most common form of psychic attack, and it can occur both intentionally and unintentionally. There was a belief that if someone was cross-eyed, possessed a squint, or had some other abnormality to the eye, he or she could unintentionally harm others by simply looking at them.

When I was growing up, I knew a girl who had eyes of different colors. One was deep blue, and the other was emerald green. I thought the combination was attractive, but in the past she would have been accused of possessing the evil eye.

Hunchbacks, dwarves, and people with eyebrows that met in the middle were also believed to have the evil eye. Emperor Napoleon III of France, King Alphonso XIII of Spain, and the English poet Lord Byron were all said to possess the evil eye.

Even two popes suffered from this affliction. Shortly after his investiture as pope, Pius IX (1792–1878) was being escorted through Rome in an open carriage. He happened to glance at a nurse holding a child at a window. A few minutes later, the child fell to its death. After this catastrophe, almost everything Pope Pius IX blessed created misfortune. He was succeeded by Pope Leo XIII (1810–1903). A large number of cardinals died while he led the Catholic Church, and this was said to be because he had the evil eye.

Some animals also have the ability to hurt people by unintentionally looking at them with an evil eye.

There have been a number of recorded instances of people who unintentionally caused harm because they were afflicted with the evil eye. Two interesting examples were recorded in the trial of three Malmesbury, Wiltshire, England witches in 1672. A farmer from Christian Malford, near Chippenham, had inadvertently killed his own cattle "by his natural evil look." Mr. Snigg, another nearby farmer, had children who were extremely thin and lacking in energy. This was attributed to Mr. Snigg's unfortunate eyes.[9]

In their book *About Yorkshire*, Thomas and Katharine Macquoid mention a case of a man who "always walked about with his eyes fixed on the ground, and never looked at any one to whom he spoke; his glance was cursed, and he dare not speak to one of his rosy children, lest some blight should fall."[10]

First thing every morning, another Yorkshire man would open his door and glance at a pear tree outside his house. This was because it was thought that the evil eye was most dangerous in the early hours of the day. As long as he did this, he would not cast an evil eye on his friends or neighbors. Over a period of time, the unfortunate tree slowly died.[11]

Even William Shakespeare referred to the evil eye. In *Love's Labour's Lost*, Lord Berowne says, "They have the plague, and caught it of your eyes" (5.2.421).

The evil eye is usually cast deliberately. If someone looks at someone else with feelings of jealousy, malice, spite, or envy, he or she can consciously harm that person. The saying "If looks could kill . . ." has a great deal of truth behind it. Even today, most people feel uncomfortable if someone stares at them. The feeling of unease increases if the stare is malevolent or spiteful.

To make matters worse, even the gods sometimes looked enviously at human beings, creating additional worries.

Belief in the evil eye is extremely old. Five-thousand-year-old Sumerian and Assyrian cuneiform texts have been discovered that discuss the evil eye and suggest possible remedies. The ancient Egyptians, Greeks, and Romans were afraid of the evil eye and used cosmetics for protection. Cosmetics were considered to possess magical qualities, and *kohl* (eye shadow) and lipstick were worn to prevent the evil eye from entering their eyes and mouths.[12] The evil eye is also mentioned in the Bible. Proverbs 23:6 says: "Eat thou not the bread of him that hath an evil eye."

It makes no difference if the evil eye is caused intentionally or unintentionally, as the result is the same: misfortune, ill health, or even death. Impotence and frigidity were commonly ascribed to the evil eye.

The weakest and most vulnerable members of the community were most likely to be harmed by the evil eye. Consequently, young animals and children were believed to be most at risk.

Belief in the evil eye is still common in Mediterranean countries such as Italy and Turkey, and it also exists in Mexico and parts of Central America. Not surprisingly, a large number of remedies have been used to avert the effects of the evil eye. Amulets of different sorts have always been the most popular. Amulets in the shape of a phallus have been used in Italy since Roman times to avert the evil eye. Even today, men in Italy will grab at their crotches when exposed to the evil eye. Another common remedy related to the phallus is to make a *figa* with the hand by clenching it in a fist with the thumb protruding between the index and middle fingers. The thumb represents the phallus. Another instant remedy that can be made by the hands is to hold up the index and little finger to create "horns." The ancient Greeks and Romans also used saliva, and even today some people in Mediterranean countries spit when exposed to the evil eye. In Greece and Turkey, a hand-crafted blue glass eye charm called a *nazar bonjuk* is still used today to repel the evil eye. Although now sold to tourists as souvenirs, locals still take them seriously, and it is rare to see an infant in public without one.

In many parts of the world, if someone praised someone or something, it was common to immediately say a word charm to counteract it. For more than four thousand years, Jewish people have said the words *kayn aynhorah*, which is Yiddish for "May no evil eye harm you." The blessing that priests give at the end of a church service is, to all intents and purposes, a protective word charm. The ancient Greeks used many word, or spoken, charms for a variety of purposes. Homer, for instance, wrote that Autolycus's sons bound a wound in the leg of Odysseus while reciting a word charm to help staunch the blood (*Odyssey* 19:457–459). This was a common practice at the time, as people believed many illnesses were caused by demons, and word charms were a popular form of protection.

Spoken charms became popular in Europe in the Middle Ages, and many Christian prayers were adapted and modified to act as charms. Even today, many superstitious people say a few words, such as "as God will" or "God bless it" whenever they or something belonging to them is complimented.[13]

Horse brasses used to be common in the United Kingdom but are seldom seen today, except as artifacts in museums. The earliest horse brasses were made from hand-hammered sheets of brass. They were circular or crescent in shape, and contained a simple design, often based on the rays of the sun. Their original purpose was to protect the animal from the evil eye. The bright, highly polished brass deflected any negativity away from the animal.

In southern Europe, bells and brightly colored ribbons were also tied to animals to protect them from the evil eye. In his book *The Evil Eye*, published in 1895, Frederick Thomas Elworthy described the amulets he saw on Neapolitan carthorses. These ranged from bells, ribbons, horns, and pheasants' feathers to horse brasses engraved with saints and angels.[14]

Special protection is necessary for children, as the forces of evil are always interested in the young, especially those who are intelligent and attractive. Protection had to be done as soon as someone praised a baby or child. In the East, the remedy was to say the opposite. A beautiful child would be described as ugly and an intelligent child would be labeled ignorant in an attempt to confuse the evil forces. Chinese parents would often comment on their children first, saying something along the lines of "My miserable, wretched, and ugly offspring" to avoid any possibility of the evil eye. In southern Russia, mothers would order their children to make a sign of the *figa* behind the back of the person who complimented them.[15] In the Middle East, small boys were sometimes dressed in girls' clothes, again in an attempt to confuse the Devil.

Various plants were used in different parts of the world to avert the evil eye. In England, people planted jack beans, believing they would protect their gardens. Garlic was popular in Greece, shamrock was used in Ireland, and barley was a popular remedy in

India. To avert the evil eye in Europe, you could say, "Here's garlic in your eyes."[16]

Vervain is a useful herb that can be used in many ways. A spray of vervain attached to the front door of your home will provide protection and prevent any negativity from entering. In addition, if someone looks enviously at anything you own, you can rub the object with a few leaves of vervain to remove the effects of the evil eye.

Crossing your fingers is considered a useful remedy if you come across someone who you suspect has the evil eye. You must not let the person see you doing this. Once the person has left, you can spit on the ground for additional protection.

Psychic protection is still necessary today. In the Western world, few people still believe in the evil eye, but everyone is surrounded by anger, negativity, jealousy, stresses of different sorts, and many other concerns. Occasionally, someone will deliberately make a psychic attack on someone they dislike or envy. Some are able to withstand the pressures of everyday life more easily than others, but even they need help from time to time. Consequently, everyone can benefit from psychic protection.

In the next few chapters, we'll look at the main remedies used for psychic protection.

Talismans, Amulets, and Charms

Several methods of psychic protection have stood the test of time. These include hand gestures such as making the sign of the *figa* (clenching the hand in a fist with the thumb protruding between the first and second fingers), wearing amulets and charms, spreading salt, using fragrances, and strengthening the aura.

Arguably, the oldest method is the use of amulets, charms, and talismans. Although these may seem like synonyms, each has a slightly different meaning. Talismans provide active power, amulets provide passive protection, and charms attract good luck and protection against bad luck.

Talismans

The origin of talismans is unknown, though they probably date back to the Stone Age. Originally, talismans were objects made from parts of animals, such as an eagle feather or a shark tooth. These provided protection and also gave the owner some of the qualities of the animal from which it came.

Talismans of this sort are still used, but it is more usual for a talisman to be created especially for its owner rather than using a found object. These talismans are intended to give the wearer special benefits. They provide power and energy as well as protection. Examples of these, dating back to Paleolithic and Neolithic times, still survive. Instructions on how to make and use talismans have been found in Egyptian papyri.

The Jewish mezuzah, still used today, is a good example of an early talisman. The mezuzah protects the home and is derived from some words of instruction in the Bible: "And thou shall write them upon the posts of thy house and on thy gates" (Deuteronomy 6:9). The mezuzah is a hollow tube that contains a sheet of parchment containing the words "Hear, O Israel, the Lord our God is One." The mezuzah is nailed to the doorpost of the house to consecrate and bless it. The occupants kiss or touch the mezuzah whenever they pass it.

In the first century CE, Appolonius of Tyana was said to have a talisman to eliminate all the scorpions in Antioch. He buried a bronze image of a scorpion and placed a pillar over it. All the scorpions left.[1]

Catherine de Medici (1519–1589) commissioned a talisman that gave her clairvoyant powers. It was formed from several metals that were mixed together at specific astrological times. Her talisman was destroyed after her death, but a copy of it can be seen at the Bibliothèque Nationale de France in Paris.

Talismans need not be made from expensive metals. I have seen people in Hong Kong using photographs and photocopies of books and computers to help them become more academic. They usually keep these in their wallets and purses, so they can look at and handle them whenever they have a spare moment.

Bells have been used as both amulets and talismans for thousands of years. According to the Bible, bells were attached to the hem of Aaron's robes to act as protective amulets (Exodus 28:33–35). Iron was considered an enemy of Satan. People also believed that Satan was frightened of the sounds that bells make. Consequently, the sound of church bells not only summons people to church but at the same time frightens Satan and his helpers. This is why bells were commonly attached to animals and children's toys in medieval times.

The Seal of Solomon, also known as the Star of David, is arguably the most famous talisman of all. This is a six-pointed star created by two overlapping triangles. The triangle that points upwards symbolizes fire, the sky, and masculinity. The downward-pointing triangle symbolizes water, earth, and femininity. The Seal of Solomon provides universal protection for anyone who wears it. As the Star of David, these interlocking triangles symbolize the nation of Israel and the Jewish religion.

Some years ago, I visited the Würzburg Mainfraken Museum in Germany and saw a talisman found on the body of Count Anselm, bishop of Würzburg, after his death in 1749. This talisman, crudely drawn on parchment, contained the six-pointed star, along with six characters, probably astrological symbols.

In the original Hebrew, the Star of David is called the Shield of David. This is because the star shielded people from negative energies.

During the Middle Ages, the Tetragrammaton was a popular talisman that protected the wearer from enemies and also attracted peace, close friendships, and longevity. The Tetragrammaton, which means "the four letters" in Greek, is the four Hebrew consonants (YHWH) that early Jewish writers used instead of writing the unspeakable name of God. The Tetragrammaton is often pronounced as Yahweh. However, observant Jews do not pronounce the name at all. Whenever it is found in the scriptures, they use the name *Adonai* ("Lord") instead. The talisman was usually in the form of a pentacle, with the five syllables of the Tetragrammaton inscribed in each corner.

Amulets

Amulets are intended to provide protection and to ward off illness and ill fortune. Amulets are passive and react to events and circumstances in the owner's life. Like talismans, amulets were originally made from natural objects. Four-leaf clovers and "lucky" rabbit feet are examples of this type of amulet. However, it didn't take people long to discover that man-made objects, especially body adornments, worked well as protective amulets. Pieces of jewelry are frequently used as amulets. St. Jude is generally considered the patron saint of policemen; in the early twentieth century, many New York police officers carried a St. Jude medal with them as a protective amulet.

Abracadabra

Nowadays, the word *abracadabra* is usually considered a nonsense word used by conjurers when performing magic tricks. The origins of this amulet are not known, but the first written reference to it, with instructions on how to use it, was included in a poem by Quintus Serenus Sammonicus, who was physician to Emperor Severus on his expedition to Britain in 208 CE.

In the Middle Ages, it was considered a powerful amulet against fevers and all negative energies. The word *abracadabra* is written eleven times, with one letter dropped each time. This creates a triangular shape that symbolizes the Holy Trinity.

```
A  B  R  A  C  A  D  A  B  R  A
  A  B  R  A  C  A  D  A  B  R
   A  B  R  A  C  A  D  A  B
    A  B  R  A  C  A  D  A
     A  B  R  A  C  A  D
      A  B  R  A  C  A
       A  B  R  A  C
        A  B  R  A
         A  B  R
          A  B
           A
```

This amulet is usually drawn on parchment paper, worn or kept for nine days, and then discarded. Ideally, it is disposed of by tossing the paper backwards over your left shoulder before sunrise into a stream that flows from east to west. There is a reason for this procedure. The left side is related to the Devil, and the amulet is disposed of before sunrise into a river flowing in the direction of the rising sun. The light of the rising sun banishes all the negative energies absorbed by the amulet.

Acorn

The acorn has been used as a protective amulet since druidic times. The druids worshiped in sacred groves of oak trees. The oracle of Dodona in ancient Greece was situated in an oak forest. The ancient Romans made crowns of oak leaves to symbolize courage and bravery.

Even today, some people place acorns on window ledges to protect the occupants of the house. The acorn is also considered to be a charm that attracts good luck and longevity.

Ankh

The origin of the ankh, a cross with a loop instead of a vertical line in the upper half, is unknown. However, it has been used as a protective amulet since Egyptian times.

Coral

Because coral looks like the branches of a tree, it is able to share the symbolism of both water and trees. Red coral also symbolizes blood, the sign of life and ultimately the soul. The ancient Romans used red coral to ward off evil spirits and the evil eye. Ornaments and jewelry made of coral still serve as amulets today.

Cross

The cross is usually considered an adornment people wear to proclaim their Christian faith. However, people have worn them as protective amulets for thousands of years. Christians started using the cross as an identifying symbol after Emperor Constantine allegedly saw one in a vision in 312 CE, shortly before winning a major battle.

In the Middle Ages, people carried disk-shaped wax amulets showing a lamb in front of the cross to protect them from magical enchantments. This amulet, known as *Agnus Dei* ("Lamb of God"), became so popular that a papal bull was passed in 1471, granting sole manufacturing rights to the pope. This amulet is still a highly lucrative source of revenue for the Roman Catholic Church today.[2] I find this fascinating, as the church originally condemned the use of amulets.

Dime

Coins are normally carried as lucky charms, but the American silver dime is an exception as it is carried as a protective amulet. Dimes containing 90 percent silver and 10 percent copper were minted until 1966, though the coins made in 1965 and 1966 are dated 1964. Silver dimes are believed to turn black when someone curses you. This belief comes from the old custom of placing silver dimes in shoes. Cursing, or hexing, powder usually contains sulfur. If someone secretly placed cursing powder in your shoes, the sulfur would turn the coin black.

While sulfur is the main component in cursing powder, graveyard dirt, salt, red pepper, and a ground-up snakeskin or powdered insect are also added to the mix. Known as "goofer's dust" in voodoo, its sole purpose is to put a curse on someone.

Jade

In the East, jade has always been considered one of the most powerful protective amulets, and business-people regularly hold jade amulets while involved in important business negotiations.[3] Green jade is associated with fertility and expansion. Jade is worn to protect the wearer from ill health and to promote restful sleep and feelings of happiness and well-being.

Knots

A common belief all around the world is that evil spirits can be caught in knots. Consequently, knots have always been used as amulets to protect people from evil spirits and other forms of harm. Knotted fringes are commonly found on church altars. The fringe confuses evil spirits, while the knots trap them and prevent them from causing harm.

Parik-tils

When I lived in Cornwall, England, in my early twenties, I became familiar with Parik-tils, or blessing holders, used by gypsies as protective amulets. Parik-tils are small drawstring bags containing a variety of small objects such as acorns, coins, feathers, herbs, stones, and pieces of paper containing spells or words of wisdom. The objects chosen were selected to match the purpose the bag was made for. Parik-tils are usually amulets to provide protection from the evil eye and any other form of negativity. However, they can also be made as talismans to attract good health, longevity, love, and prosperity.

Sator Arepo Magic Square

The Sator Arepo magic square is a famous amulet dating from Roman times. Several of them have been found in mosaics at a number of Roman sites, including Pompeii and Cirencester in England. The exact meaning of the words in the magic square is not known, as the word *arepo* is not Latin. However, most experts hypothesize that the square reads: "Sator, the sower, holds the wheels by his work."[4] The Sator Arepo magic square is drawn on parchment, and carried as a protective amulet.

```
S   A   T   O   R
A   R   E   P   O
T   E   N   E   T
O   P   E   R   A
R   O   T   A   S
```

This square can be read from left to right, in the usual way. It can also be read vertically, in columns. In addition, it can also be read in reverse, both horizontally and vertically.

Witch's Ladder

A witch's ladder is a length of ribbon or cord braided or knotted to hold small objects such as feathers, shells, beads, small bells, and crystals. To make a witch's ladder you'll need some lengths of white and blue cord or ribbon. Eighteen inches is a good length to start with. You can use as many lengths of cord as you wish for braiding. However, unless you are experienced at braiding, it is a good idea to start with three pieces. Once you have made one witch's ladder, you can be as ambitious as you like when you make more.

Traditionally, a witch's ladder is made over a period of time, usually during a lunar month. However, you can make your ladder at any time you wish, as long as you create it the same time of day each time and spread it over a specific length of time, such as a week or a month. You can, if necessary, make a witch's ladder in one session, but it gains strength by being made over a period of time.

When you are ready to start, gather all the materials you'll need on a table. Include the lengths of ribbon and the objects you intend inserting into the ladder. You might want candle wax to seal the ends of your ladder. Alternatively, you might tie one end of the ladder to a ring or into a loop, so it can be easily hung from a hook or nail.

Braid some of the cords together, and then insert one of the objects you have selected. Small bells are especially useful for witches' ladders that are intended for protection purposes. Some objects, such as feathers, can be braided into the ladder, while others are tied on or attached in some other way. Think about your need and desire for protection as you braid your ladder. Once you have attached an object to your ladder, put it away carefully until your next session. You might be in a hurry to complete the ladder, but it will be more powerful and work better if done in stages.

Finish the ladder by blessing it and thanking it for protecting you. Kiss it, and then hang it somewhere in your home and let it do its work.

Making a witch's ladder is part of a folk tradition called cord or knot magic. Another example of knot magic is included in chapter 13.

Lucky Charms

Lucky charms are intended to attract good luck and good fortune to whoever owns them. Because of this, they combine some of the qualities of both talismans and amulets, and are frequently used to provide protection and good luck for purposes other than simply their owner's well-being.

A well-known example of this occurred in 1968, when the contractors working on the Vanguard rocket project for the United States Navy attributed the numerous failures to the absence of St. Christopher medals on the rockets. St. Christopher is considered the patron saint of travelers, and many people carry one when traveling away from home. A medal was attached to the next rocket, and it performed perfectly.[5]

Almost anything can be used as a lucky charm. Buttons and coins are frequently carried as charms. Many people collect small charms and wear them on a charm bracelet. The best lucky charms are those that are given to you, as they carry the love and friendship the giver has for you.

The four-leaf clover is arguably the best-known lucky charm, and most people have looked for one at some time or another. An old rhyme tells how each leaf represents a different aspect of life:

One leaf is for fame
And one leaf is for wealth

And one is for a faithful lover
And one to bring you glorious health
Are all in the four-leaved clover.

If you find a four-leaf clover, make sure you keep it. It is thought that you'll attract bad luck if you give it away.

Chestnuts

Chestnuts are commonly carried as a lucky charm. This is not surprising, as they are smooth and pleasant to hold and fondle. Chestnuts are long-living trees, and carrying a chestnut is thought to give the person some of the tree's good health and luck.

How to Use Lucky Charms

Charms are worn or carried to attract good luck to the owner. Usually, they are not purified or treated in any way before use. I seldom carry any lucky charms around with me, but if I did, I would purify them first, to eliminate any undesirable energies they may have picked up before coming into my possession.

Amulets and talismans need to be treated before they can be used for protection purposes. Amulets are purified using at least one of the four traditional elements of fire, earth, air, and water.

Some people like to purify their amulets using all four elements. This is not always possible, though. An amulet made of paper, for instance, may not sur-

vive being purified by fire. I like to use all four elements when practical but sometimes have to settle
for one, if circumstances demand it.

Although you should have fun when purifying
your amulets, you need to focus on what you are
doing, and treat the process with respect. A casual,
flippant approach is likely to do more harm than
good.

There are two ways to purify your amulet with
fire. You can buy a white candle and pass your amulet through the flame. The candle should not have
been used for any other purpose beforehand and
should be discarded once you have purified your
amulet(s). The other method is to choose a bright,
sunny day and expose your amulet to the sun for
several hours. Both methods work equally well.

There are three ways to purify your amulet using
the element of earth. You can bury your amulet in
dry earth and leave it overnight. You can also make a
small circle of stones outdoors, place your amulet in
the center, and leave it there overnight. Alternatively,
you can bury your amulet in salt for twenty-four
hours. The salt should not have been used for any
other purpose beforehand and should be discarded
afterwards.

There are also three ways to purify your amulet using the element of air. You can take your amulet outdoors on a nice day. Face east, and hold your amulet

as high as you can in both hands for thirty seconds. Repeat, facing the south, west, and north directions. You might prefer to light a white candle and pass your amulet through the smoke it produces. Incense is frequently used for this, too. Finally, you can take several slow, deep breaths. Hold your amulet in your cupped hands and exhale over it.

You can purify your amulet using the element of water by washing it under running water. Ordinary tap water can be used, but it's better to use spring or stream water. Allow the amulet to dry naturally in the fresh air. If the material of the amulet does not allow you to wash it under running water, you can sprinkle a few drops of rainwater over it. If necessary, you can immediately dry the amulet with tissues or a soft towel.

Trust your intuition and listen to what your amulet or charm tells you. You might intend using all four elements but find you "know" your amulet is purified after one or two elements.

There are several methods to consecrate a talisman for its purpose. One simple but effective method involves holding your talisman in your cupped hands twice a day, usually the morning and evening. Gaze at the talisman and focus all your energies onto it. Think about what you want the talisman to do for you. Concentrate on this for as long as you can, and stop as soon as your mind starts wandering. Wrap the talisman in silk, and keep it in a safe place until it is time to repeat the process. Continue doing this for as many days as necessary. Your talisman will let you know when it is fully charged. You will notice its distinctive energy as soon as it reaches this state. Once this occurs, your talisman is ready for use.[6]

Talismans, amulets, and charms are all important items for protection purposes. However, they are not the only ones. In the next chapter, we'll look at a less obvious form of protection: scents, perfumes, and flower essences.

three

Scents, Perfumes, and Flower Essences

People have used scents of various sorts throughout human history. Sumerian, Babylonian, Chal-
dean, Canaanite, Hebrew, and Egyptian priests all
made use of incense in their rituals.[1] Because odors
and fragrances can alter our perceptions and feelings,
they have always been associated with magic. Thousands of years ago, Egyptian priests were experts at
combining different scents in their incenses to create the desired spiritual effects in people attending
their rituals and ceremonies. They also believed that

burning incense helped them maintain a close relationship with the gods.

Many years ago, a friend performed a fascinating experiment with members of a club we both belonged to. At each meeting, she used different aromatherapy oils. No one except her had any idea which one she would choose. Each scent affected the meeting in different ways. Some made us excitable and exuberant, others made us quiet and inward-looking. I found the experiment fascinating, as it clearly demonstrated the effects that different smells have on us.

Humans don't use the sense of smell nearly as much today as they did thousands of years ago. The saying "to smell danger," for instance, had more than just a metaphoric use; it enabled people to escape potentially difficult situations.

Ancient Egyptians used perfume when embalming the dead and believed that the soul ascended to heaven in a cloud of incense. The three kings who came to visit the baby Jesus brought him gifts of the precious, sweet-smelling aromatic gums frankincense and myrrh, still widely used in incense for Christian rituals.

Perfumes act on the olfactory nerves in the nose, which stimulate the brain, arousing strong emotions. Not surprisingly, some perfumes work well as aphrodisiacs.

Many people believe that perfume clears the brain. Napoleon Bonaparte always immersed his head into a bowl of eau de cologne before the start of a battle.[2] Pleasant smells awaken the senses and subconsciously remind us of happy and positive feelings. Scientists have demonstrated that pleasant scents create feelings of surprise and joy, while unpleasant smells create feelings of disgust and unhappiness.[3] Because of this, you should always keep your home well-aired and place fragrant flowers in the areas you frequent.

Because different scents have such a profound effect, many of them can be used for protection purposes when necessary.

Here are some you might like to experiment with:

Acacia

The scent of acacia relaxes, soothes, and eliminates worries and other concerns. It is also believed to attract good luck.

Ambretta

The ambretta plant produces large yellow flowers with crimson centers. It has a long-lasting scent that enhances peace in the home. It is good for all family relationships and enables people to get along well.

Angelica

Angelica is sometimes placed in children's beds to provide protection while they sleep. Angelica enhances feelings of independence and confidence.

Basil

The scent of basil eases feelings of anxiety and concern. This makes it the perfect scent for chronic worriers. Basil enables people to see other people's point of view and to speak diplomatically. It also enhances a person's intuition.

Bay

The Delphic Oracle in ancient Greece was said to use bay to enhance intuition. Bay diffuses negativity, promotes peace and well-being, and enhances psychic perception.

Bergamot

Bergamot provides confidence and motivation and also promotes feelings of well-being and happiness. It stimulates the heart and soul and provides peace of mind.

Carnation

Carnation provides courage and vitality. It enables people to stand up for themselves and to handle situations that may otherwise be stressful.

Cedar Wood

The scent of cedar wood is comforting and increases feelings of positivity and happiness. It enhances home and family life. Cedar wood provides willpower, determination, and courage.

Chamomile

The scent of chamomile eliminates negativity and allows people to let go of long-held grievances. It dissolves criticism of both self and others, and stimulates new ways of looking at old situations.

Champaca

Michelia champaca is an evergreen tree native to Southern Asia. It produces an aromatic scent that eases feelings of negativity and anxiety, and replaces them with feelings of positivity, well-being, and happiness. Because of this, the plant is sometimes known as the "joy perfume tree."

Cistus

Cistus has a scent similar to amber.[4] Its scent encourages thoughts of positivity and happiness, and makes people feel more optimistic about the future.

Cinnamon

True cinnamon is known as Ceylon cinnamon and is not the same as the more readily available mass-market cinnamon, which is actually cassia tree bark.

Although cassia bark has a stronger taste and scent than Ceylon cinnamon, it does not have the same effect on your mind and spirit as true cinnamon. This scent helps people regain their zest and passion for life. It eliminates introversion and enables people to be more friendly, outgoing, and sociable. It enables people to see what life is like when they release their inhibitions and act freely and openly.

Citronella

Citronella encourages feelings of boldness and bravery. It creates vitality and feelings of optimism about the future.

Clary Sage

Clary sage centers the soul and enhances creativity. It is a relaxing scent that promotes sleep and pleasant dreams.

Clove

The scent of clove creates feelings of relaxation and enables people to explore new and different possibilities. It provides release from outmoded ways of thinking and allows people to let go of thoughts— and even possessions and acquaintances—holding them back.

Clover
The delicate scent of clover calms the mind, reduces anxiety, and promotes happiness and harmony.

Cumin
The scent of cumin encourages clear thinking and a positive approach to life. It is a useful scent when you are facing adversity. Cumin is also believed to strengthen the bonds between husband and wife.

Cypress
The scent of cypress provides protection and support when moving forward into new and uncharted territory. It enables people to move out of their comfort zone, see new opportunities, and move forward confidently in a new direction.

Eucalyptus
The scent of eucalyptus allows people to release the mistakes and regrets of the past, and to move forward again with a sense of joy and freedom. Eucalyptus promotes feelings of lightness, spontaneity, and good humor.

Fennel
The scent of fennel gives people confidence to achieve specific goals, aim higher than ever before, and be assertive in a positive way. Fennel provides courage, stamina, and persistence.

Frankincense

Frankincense provides protection against stress, strain, and worry. It enables you to aim high, while keeping your feet firmly on the ground. It enhances wisdom and the desire to learn and grow. Frankincense is useful for meditation and for enhancing spirituality.

Gardenia

The scent of gardenia helps people stand up for what is honest and true. It also strengthens the bonds between family members.

Geranium

The scent of geranium soothes emotional ups and downs and helps people regain balance and a sense of control over their lives. It enables workaholics to know when to pause and relax, and to allow more joy in their lives.

Grapefruit

The scent of grapefruit is emotionally purifying. It creates feelings of optimism and joy, while at the same time eliminates negative thoughts, feelings, and frustrations. It enables people to look at everything from a fresh point of view.

Hawthorn
The pleasant scent of hawthorn promotes feelings of calmness and protects you from other people's negativity and ill-humor.

Heliotrope
The scent of heliotrope enhances spirituality and intuition. It raises the spirits and encourages everyone pursuing a spiritual path.

Honeysuckle
The subtle scent of honeysuckle soothes troubled nerves, and enables people to look at difficult situations calmly and rationally.

Hyacinth
Hyacinth is an especially useful scent as it helps people to believe in themselves. It provides calmness, confidence, and optimism.

Iris
The scent of iris encourages feelings of well-being, and enables people to communicate better with others. It provides calmness and peace of mind.

Jasmine
The scent of jasmine encourages feelings of balance, harmony, cooperation, and the ability to get along well with others. Jasmine also stimulates positive

ideas, making it particularly useful for anyone engaged in creative pursuits.

Juniper

The scent of juniper eliminates negativity, both in people and in the home. It enables people to think ahead and make positive, constructive plans for the future.

Lavender

Lavender is a calming scent that enhances feelings of relaxation and harmony. It nurtures and revitalizes the mind, body, and soul. Lavender provides protection from the negativity and verbal attacks of others. It also provides the necessary strength and confidence to help people move ahead again.

Lemon

The scent of lemon eliminates feelings of negativity, and encourages thinking before acting. Lemon stimulates the mind and eliminates nervous tension. It enables people to let go of doubt and worry, providing time and space to think logically and clearly.

Lemongrass

The scent of lemongrass enables people to expand their self-created boundaries and limitations, and enables them to move forward with feelings of confidence and optimism. It aids concentration and enhances intuition.

Lily

The scent of lily enhances intuition and is believed to create good luck. It encourages spiritual thoughts and nurtures all relationships.

Lily of the Valley

The scent of lily of the valley provides feelings of security, safety, well-being, and abundance. It encourages people to help others without any thought of reward.

Lime

The scent of lime eliminates stress and frustrations. It is especially useful for people who find it hard to relax and unwind. It also provides protection from infectious illnesses. It encourages perseverance and the hard work necessary to achieve worthwhile goals.

Marjoram

Marjoram releases anxiety and self-sabotaging thoughts and feelings. It is especially useful for people who tend to look on the negative side of life rather than the positive. It provides feelings of protection and support when required.

Mimosa

The scent of mimosa creates feelings of confidence and optimism. It eliminates negative emotions and enhances the ability to forgive others.

Myrrh

Myrrh has a slightly bitter scent. It was one of the perfumes carried by the three wise men who made the pilgrimage to see the infant Jesus. Consequently, it is used to enhance spirituality and is especially useful for people who wish to meditate at a deeper, more spiritual level.

Myrtle

The fragrant scent of myrtle encourages people to look ahead, to make plans for the future, and to remain positive no matter what is going on in their lives. Myrtle purifies the mind, body, and spirit.

Narcissus

Narcissus has a pleasing perfume that encourages tact and gentleness when dealing with others.

Nutmeg

Spicy nutmeg stimulates passion and energy. It also provides motivation and a strong desire to succeed. It enables people to conquer challenges and situations that proved difficult or impossible in the past.

Patchouli

Patchouli provides feelings of peace, cooperation, and emotional balance. It enables people to handle difficult situations calmly and confidently. It also enhances close relationships.

Peppermint

The scent of peppermint is stimulating and passionate. It helps people understand their true purpose in life and overcome the challenges that stand in the way of success.

Pimento

The scent of pimento invigorates the physical body and promotes positive thinking. It also provides motivation and enthusiasm.

Pine

The scent of pine enables people to recognize their true worth. It helps them to let go of the past and to live in the present, free of guilt and other negative baggage. It enhances feelings of happiness and well-being.

Rose

The scent of rose brings good luck into the house. It aids the body, mind, and soul and enhances all close relationships. It nurtures people who are emotionally

withdrawn and enables them to experience friendship and love.

Rosemary

Rosemary is a purifying herb, and its fragrance increases confidence and self-esteem. It enhances creativity and enables people to believe they can achieve
anything they set their minds upon.

Sandalwood

Some temples in India have been constructed from
sandalwood and are reputed to have retained their
scent for centuries. Sandalwood trees are all owned
by the Indian government, and harvesting is strictly
controlled. Consequently, sandalwood is expensive.
In Buddhism, sandalwood is used to enable a person to remain alert during meditation. The *tilaka*,
a line or mark found on the foreheads of Hindu
priests and women, is frequently made from sandalwood paste. The tilaka symbolizes the third eye
and is related to a number of Hindu deities, as well
as spiritual enlightenment. A tilaka is usually worn
on special days such as a birthday, wedding, or holy
day.

The scent of sandalwood enables people to remain calm and protected, even in difficult situations.
It repels other people's negativity and aggression. It
also gives people time to relax and contemplate the

mysteries of the universe. It helps move people toward enlightenment.

Tarragon

The scent of tarragon provides confidence and a sense of responsibility. It enables people to see new possibilities and challenges that were not available before.

Thyme

The scent of thyme increases domestic harmony. It provides energy and enthusiasm, and motivates people to aim high. It also provides strength and willpower when necessary.

Verbena

The scent of verbena provides courage in difficult or stressful situations. It encourages people to stand on their own two feet and resist unwelcome advances by others.

Vetiver

The scent of vetiver keeps people grounded and in contact with Mother Earth. It is a stabilizing, protective fragrance that recharges all the cells of the body.

Violet

The scent of violet has been related to longevity. It provides energy, vitality, and a sense of fun and play.

How to Use the Fragrances

The easiest way to obtain the benefits of these fragrances is to buy them as essential oils. Essential oils are fragrances obtained from various parts of different plants. Unfortunately, true essential oils are expensive because a large number of plants are required to make a small amount of oil. For instance, it takes between thirty and forty roses to make a single drop of rose essential oil. Synthetic oils are much cheaper, but do not provide the same benefits as genuine essential oils. For something as important as protection, it is vital that you purchase genuine essential oils.

The oils can be used in a variety of ways. Electric oil burners can be purchased at any store that sells aromatherapy supplies. They are safe and easy to use. You might prefer the mystery and romance of a candle burner. However, you should never leave a candle unattended. I love candles but usually use an electric burner, as it is safer and more convenient.

You might prefer to absorb the oil as an inhalant. Add five drops of the oil of your choice to a bowl of boiling water. Place a towel over your head and the bowl, and absorb the vapor for two or three minutes. You may prefer to absorb the oil by putting a few drops onto a handkerchief and holding it a few inches away from your nose for a few minutes.

One of the most pleasant ways to enjoy the oil or oils of your choice is to prepare a bath. To avoid dirtying the bath, you need to dilute the oil of your choice with a water-soluble dispersing bath oil base. You will be able to buy this at the same store you buy your oils from.

You can add a few drops to your sheets before going to bed. Most essential oils will not stain the sheets, though naturally, you should exercise caution when using darker oils.

You can place a few drops of essential oils in the corner of each room of your home to provide a fragrant form of protection.

I frequently place a drop or two of an essential oil onto the seat of my car to ensure I enjoy a pleasant, relaxing, and safe drive.

Incense

People have burned incense for thousands of years. In the Book of Genesis, the first book in the Bible, Noah "offered burnt offerings on the altar. And the Lord smelled a sweet savour" (Genesis 8:20–21). The Bible contains a number of other references to the burning of incense, showing how old this practice is.[5]

Originally, incense was burned as a pleasing offering to the gods. The ancient Egyptians burned incense to the sun god Ra three times a day: frankincense when the sun appeared in the morning, myrrh at midday, and *kuphi* as the sun set in the evening.

Kuphi was a combination of sixteen ingredients that was prepared by priests in a secret ritual that took months to complete. Kuphi incense brought peace and calm to everyone who breathed it. In his book *On Isis and Osiris*, Plutarch wrote, "[kyphi] is a mixture of sixteen ingredients compounded: honey, wine, raisin, galingale, resin, myrrh, thorny trefoil, hartwort, mastic, asphalt, thorn apple, dock, both kinds of juniper—they call one 'the greater' and the other 'the lesser'—cardamom, and reed. These are mixed in an orderly way, and the ointment recipes of sacred writings are read when they are being mixed."[6]

The early Christians were suspicious of the Jewish and pagan use of incense, and used it solely for purification purposes. However, from the fifth century onwards it gained in popularity and in time became a regular part of rituals in church services. This is not surprising, as it is pleasing to think your prayers are being carried up to heaven on spirals of sweet-smelling incense.

In medieval times, magicians used incense to help them conjure up spirits. Magicians today still use incense for a variety of purposes, including relaxation, achieving the right state of mind in which to perform the rituals, purifying work spaces, and creating the right atmosphere for their work.

Incense is readily available nowadays and is used mainly for purification and cleansing purposes. Manufactured incense, in the form of powder, cones, and joss sticks, is easy to find, and most people are content to use them when purifying their home and work environments.

If you are purchasing incense for psychic protection purposes, you should choose one that contains mainly herbs traditionally used for protection. The most popular of these are aloe, angelica (root), anise, balm of Gilead, basil, bay laurel, betony, caraway, chamomile, cinquefoil, clove, coriander, dill, dragon's blood, fennel, fern, garlic, hawthorn, holly, hyssop, ivy, lavender, lilac, mandrake, marjoram, meadowsweet, mistletoe, mugwort, mullein, nettle, onion, pennyroyal (don't use pennyroyal if you are pregnant), periwinkle, rose, rosemary, rowan, rue, sage, St. John's wort, sandalwood, vervain, witch hazel, and wormwood.

It is not hard to make incense, and I know several people who enjoy making their own. If this appeals to you, there are several books available that give full instruction on the art.[7]

Smudging

Smudging is an old English word that means "a smoky fire." Cattle were driven through the smoke to rid them of insects. In modern usage, the word smudging refers to the burning of herbs and spices to cleanse and purify people, ritual objects, and spaces such as the interior of homes.

The Native Americans burned sage, sweetgrass, cedar, and juniper for cleansing and purification purposes. Until comparatively recently, rural homes in the United Kingdom were cleansed with rosemary smoke on May Day. Beltane, the name of the celebrations held between sunset on April 30 and sunset on May 2, is primarily a fertility festival to celebrate the coming of summer and the fertility of the earth. Purifying the home at this time was intended to protect it, remove any negativity that may be present, and make it ready for the new season.

You can smudge your own home using single herbs or a mixture of your choosing. Traditionally, sagebrush and rosemary were used to cleanse and purify a home. Place the herbs in a fireproof bowl. As herbs create plenty of heat, you should choose your container carefully. Light the herbs and gently fan the smoke to encourage it to rise up and fill your home with a sweet-smelling scent. Make sure you leave at least one window open. This symbolically allows any negative energy to escape.

For convenience, most people use a bundle of herbs tied together, rather than burning herbs in a container. This bundle of herbs is called a smudge stick. You can hold this and walk around the house with it, to make sure that every room receives its share of smoke.

While cleansing the home, make sure to wash yourself and other members of the family in the smoke. It is easy to do this with a smudge stick. Start at the outside of the person's left foot and move the smoke up the left leg and body. Smudge both sides of the left arm and then continue to the top of the head, before moving downwards again to the outside of the right foot.

You can also smudge your home with a smudging spray that contains sage, cedar, lavender, marjoram and pine. "Smudge in Spray" is available at most New Age stores and also from the manufacturer, Crystal Garden, Inc. (www.thecrystalgarden.com).

You do not need to wait until May 1 to smudge your home. You can do it whenever there has been discord in the home or when you feel the need to rid your home of negativity.

four

Crystals and Gemstones

Crystals and gemstones have been valued throughout human history. For thousands of years, people
have used them for adornment, healing, and as talismans and protective amulets. The bright colors and
rarity of precious stones must have captivated early
people, and many gems have been found in ancient
tombs. They were probably buried with people to
protect them as they traveled to the next world.

It's fascinating to think that ancient people adorned
themselves with necklaces and earrings long before

they thought about wearing clothes.[1] From crowns, diadems, and tiaras on the head to toe rings and ankle bracelets on the feet, early people decorated almost every part of their bodies with precious stones.

The ancient Egyptians used gemstone amulets extensively. Archaeologists working on an ancient tomb at Shêch Abd el-Qurna, dating back some 3,500 years, found the mummy of a young woman, presumably of noble birth. She wore a necklace containing four rows of beads, consisting of pendants of gods and a selection of sacred symbols. She also wore two smaller necklaces of gold, lapis lazuli, and carnelian; two large earrings containing precious jewels; a scarab ring; a gold belt (again containing lapis lazuli and carnelian); and a gold bracelet. Her large necklace was obviously a powerful protective amulet.[2]

King Tutankhamun ruled Egypt approximately 3,300 years ago. When the young king's tomb was discovered in 1922, archaeologists found a wealth of amulets, bracelets, rings, collars, and breastplates made of gold and set with precious stones. Numerous books attest to the magnificent skill and workmanship of the artists who created them.

In ancient Egypt, certain stones were used for specific amulets, and there are many examples of these in the *Book of the Dead*. Lapis lazuli, for instance, was frequently carved into the shape of an eye to provide protection for the dead.

Ancient Indian texts such as the *Ramayana* and *Bhagavad-Gita* describe the various adornments worn by the main characters in great detail. Each had an important religious or protective aspect. Arguably the oldest amulet in India is the *navaratna* ring, containing nine precious stones that protected the wearer from inauspicious celestial influences.

There are many references to precious stones in the Bible. Onyx is mentioned in the first book of the Bible (Genesis 2:12). Aaron's breastplate contained twelve precious stones:

> *And thou shalt make the breastplate of judgment with cunning work; after the work of the ephod thou shalt make it; of gold, of blue, and of purple, and of scarlet, and of fine twined linen, shalt thou make it.*
>
> *Foursquare it shall be being doubled; a span shall be the length thereof, and a span shall be the breadth thereof.*
>
> *And thou shalt set in it settings of stones, even four rows of stones: the first row shall be a sardius (ruby), a topaz, and a carbuncle: this shall be the first row.*
>
> *And the second row shall be an emerald, a sapphire, and a diamond* [probably jade].
>
> *And the third row a ligure* [jacinth], *an agate, and an amethyst.*

> And the fourth row a beryl, and an onyx,
> and a jasper: they shall be set in gold in their
> inclosings.
>
> And the stones shall be with the names of
> the children of Israel, twelve, according to their
> names, like the engravings of a signet; every one
> with his name shall they be according to the
> twelve tribes (Exodus 28:15–21).

In the New Testament, St. John the Divine envi-
sioned the twelve foundations of the walls of Jerusalem adorned with precious stones:

> And the building of the wall of it was of jas-
> per: and the city was pure gold, like unto clear
> glass.
>
> And the foundations of the wall of the city were
> garnished with all manner of precious stones. The
> first foundation was jasper; the second, sapphire;
> the third, a chalcedony; the fourth, an emerald;
>
> The fifth, sardonyx; the sixth, sardius; the
> seventh, chrysolite; the eighth, beryl; the ninth, a
> topaz; the tenth, a chrysoprasus; the eleventh, a
> jacinth; the twelfth, an amethyst.
>
> And the twelve gates were twelve pearls; every
> several gate was of one pearl: and the street of the
> city was pure gold, as it were transparent glass
> (Revelation 21:18–21).

In older times, people who traveled across the seas needed all the protection they could find. A third- or fourth-century Greek lapidary listed seven gemstone amulets intended to help sailors and fishermen. The first one, made from carbuncle or chalcedony, protected seamen from drowning. The second amulet was made from rock crystal or corundum. The third amulet, made with aquamarine beryl, banished fear. The fourth amulet contained an agate with a white center to provide protection from the evil eye. The fifth amulet was made from coral. This was attached to the bow of the boat to protect it in all weather conditions. The sixth amulet was probably banded agate. It provided protection from stormy conditions. The seventh amulet was possibly jet. It protected people who traveled by river or sea.[3]

Up until at least the seventeenth century, most people believed in the protective and talismanic qualities of gemstones. However, there were exceptions. When the court jester of Emperor Charles V of France was asked what the property of turquoise was, he replied, "If you should happen to fall from a high tower whilst you were wearing a turquoise on your finger, the turquoise would remain unbroken."[4]

Your Birthstone

Many people wear a gemstone related to their month of birth or zodiac sign. Usually, they are unaware of the history of this practice, or the fact that such gems can be used as protective amulets.

The custom of wearing a stone related to your date of birth is comparatively recent. This is surprising, as both Flavius Josephus, the first century Jewish historian, and St. Jerome, in the fourth century, related the twelve stones in Aaron's breastplate with the twelve signs of the zodiac. Unfortunately, different translations of the Bible list different selections of stones for Aaron's breastplate. Some of the names given in the earliest texts are not known today. It is also possible that the people living in Egypt at the time of Moses were not familiar with all of the stones named in modern translations. To complicate matters still further, two breastplates existed. The original breastplate, known as the Mosaic Breastplate, disappeared when the First Temple of Jerusalem was destroyed. Flavius Josephus examined the Breastplate of the Second Temple. It was probably made in the sixth century BCE.

According to George Frederick Kunz, the custom of wearing birthstones began in eighteenth-century Poland.[5] However, the Gemological Institute of America says the custom began in Germany about 1562.[6] Prior to this, some people owned stones for all twelve signs of the zodiac and wore them at the relevant times.

The first lists of stones for each month were based on the twelve stones mentioned by St. John the Divine. These lists began in March, because this is the first month in the pre-Julian calendar:

Month	Gemstone
March	Jasper
April	Sapphire
May	Chalcedony
June	Emerald
July	Sardonyx
August	Sardius
September	Chrysolite
October	Beryl
November	Topaz
December	Chrysoprasus
January	Jacinth
February	Amethyst

Over the years, a number of different lists were compiled. In 1912, the National Association of Jewelers compiled a list that they hoped would become the standard. Unfortunately, other jewelry trade groups created their own different lists. In 1937, the National Association of Goldsmiths of Great Britain created a list of birthstones, and the American Jewelry Industry Council adopted this in 1952. It has little in common with the original list based on the Foundation Stones, and only three of the original stones (amethyst, sardonyx [sardius], and topaz) remain in their original positions:

Month	Gemstone
January	Garnet
February	Amethyst
March	Aquamarine or bloodstone
April	Diamond (or rock crystal)
May	Emerald
June	Pearl, moonstone [or alexandrite]
July	Ruby
August	Peridot or sardonyx
September	Sapphire (or lapis lazuli)
October	Opal [or pink tourmaline]
November	Topaz [or citrine]
December	Turquoise [or zircon]

The stones in round brackets are included in the British list but are excluded from the Jewelry Industry Council's list. The stones in square brackets are in the Jewelry Industry Council's list but are not included in the British list.

Astrological Stones

In *Antiquities of the Jews,* Josephus also related the stones from Aaron's breastplate to the twelve signs of the zodiac. He did this using the colors and powers associated with the signs, and the properties associated with each stone:

Zodiac Sign	Gemstone
Aries	Bloodstone
Taurus	Sapphire
Gemini	Agate
Cancer	Emerald
Leo	Onyx
Virgo	Carnelian
Libra	Chrysolite
Scorpio	Beryl
Sagittarius	Topaz
Capricorn	Ruby
Aquarius	Garnet
Pisces	Amethyst

The ancient Greeks also related the signs of the zodiac to different gemstones. They called this study *Lithica:*

Zodiac Sign	Gemstone
Aries	Hematite
Taurus	Emerald
Gemini	Multicolored stones

Cancer	Adularia
Leo	Ruby
Virgo	Beryl
Libra	Agate
Scorpio	Amethyst
Sagittarius	Turquoise
Capricorn	Onyx
Aquarius	Amber
Pisces	Coral

Many other listings have been made over the years. Even the famed author, magician, and occultist Aleister Crowley (1875–1947) created a list:

Zodiac Sign	Gemstone
Aries	Ruby
Taurus	Topaz
Gemini	Alexandrite or tourmaline
Cancer	Amber
Leo	Cat's-eye
Virgo	Peridot
Libra	Emerald
Scorpio	Snakestone
Sagittarius	Jacinth
Capricorn	Black diamond
Aquarius	Glass
Pisces	Pearl[7]

Nowadays, with so many different lists to choose from, it makes sense to choose a stone that you happen to like, and use that as your protective birthstone. However, here are some possibilities to consider if you want to remain true to the usual accepted birthstones for your sign. If you don't like any of the gemstones associated with your sign in particular, you might like to select one from one of the two other signs that share your element. Fire signs are Aries, Leo, and Sagittarius; Earth signs are Taurus, Virgo, and Capricorn; Air signs are Gemini, Libra, and Aquarius; and Water signs are Cancer, Scorpio, and Pisces.

Aries
Bloodstone, carnelian, coral, diamond, garnet, red jasper, fire opal, quartz crystal, ruby, sardonyx

Taurus
Moss agate, carnelian, chrysoprase, coral, red coral, diamond, emerald, jade, lapis lazuli, malachite, opal, pyrite, sapphire, topaz, turquoise

Gemini
Agate, moss agate, alexandrite, aquamarine, citrine, emerald, garnet, moonstone, pearl, quartz crystal, tiger's-eye, topaz

Cancer

Agate, amber, carnelian, chalcedony, emerald, jacinth, moonstone, olivine, opal, pearl, quartz crystal, rose quartz, ruby, sapphire

Leo

Agate, amber, cat's-eye, chrysolite, diamond, garnet, jasper, onyx, peridot, ruby, sapphire, sardonyx, tiger's-eye, topaz

Virgo

Agate, moss agate, amethyst, apatite, aquamarine, aventurine, carnelian, diamond, emerald, jacinth, green jade, jasper, lapis lazuli, marble, opal, peridot, sapphire, sardonyx, turquoise, zircon

Libra

Aquamarine, aventurine, beryl, chrysolite, coral, diamond, emerald, jacinth, jade, jasper, lapis lazuli, malachite, opal, sapphire, tourmaline

Scorpio

Agate, amethyst, aquamarine, beryl, bloodstone, citrine, coral, garnet, malachite, obsidian, opal, pearl, rutilated quartz, ruby, topaz

Sagittarius

Amethyst, jacinth, lapis lazuli, obsidian, opal, peridot, sapphire, sodalite, sugilite, topaz, turquoise, zircon

Capricorn

Amethyst, azurite, beryl, bloodstone, carnelian, chrysoprase, garnet, jet, lapis lazuli, malachite, obsidian, onyx, quartz crystal, ruby, sapphire, green tourmaline, turquoise, yellow zircon

Aquarius

Amber, amethyst, aquamarine, chalcedony, white coral, rock crystal, garnet, glass, jacinth, malachite, onyx, pearl, quartz crystal, sapphire, turquoise, zircon

Pisces

Amethyst, aquamarine, bloodstone, coral, diamond, jade, jasper, moonstone, mother-of-pearl, pearl, sapphire

Gemstones for Your Day of Birth

In India, it is common to wear gemstones determined by the day of the month you were born on. For protective purposes, the stone should be in direct contact with your skin.

There are three instances where the recommended stones are replaced or restricted. Because of this, before checking your day of birth, add up the total of your month, day, and year of birth, and reduce this to a single digit. For instance, if you were born on August 12, 1988, you would add together $8 + 1 + 2 + 1 + 9 + 8 + 8$. This totals 37. As you need to reduce this to a single digit, you add the three and seven together (3 + 7 = 10). Finally, the one and the zero are added together, leaving a 1.

1, 10, 19, 28

If you were born on the first, tenth, nineteenth, or twenty-eighth of any month, the best protective stones for you are amber, carnelian, red coral, garnet, red opal, ruby, yellow sapphire, sunstone, yellow topaz, gold topaz and turquoise.

However, if the total of your month, day and year of birth reduce down to a 2, 4, 7, or 8, you should not wear red coral or ruby.

2, 11, 20, 29

If you were born on the second, eleventh, twentieth, or twenty-ninth of any month, the best protective stones are cat's-eye, green jade, moonstone, green opal, white pearl and tiger's-eye.

3, 12, 21, 30

If you were born on the third, twelfth, twenty-first, or thirtieth of any month, the best protective stones are amethyst, coral, emerald and topaz.

4, 13, 22, 31

If you were born on the fourth, thirteenth, twenty-second, or thirty-first of any month, the best protective stones are blue aquamarine, white coral, diamond, garnet, hessonite, reddish-brown or gray opal, light blue sapphire, and zircon.

5, 14, 23

If you were born on the fifth, fourteenth, or twenty-third of any month, the best protective stones are diamond, white sapphire and zircon.

6, 15, 24

If you were born on the sixth, fifteenth, or twenty-fourth of any month, the best protective stones are alexandrite, pale green aquamarine, green beryl, bloodstone, red coral, emerald, green jade, green opal, peridot, and ruby.

However, if the total of your month, day, and year of birth reduces to a 3, you should not wear emerald. Replace the emerald with either yellow sapphire or golden topaz.

7, 16, 25

If you were born on the seventh, sixteenth, or twenty-fifth of any month, the best protective stones for you are cat's-eye, green jade, moonstone, white opal, pearl, and tiger's-eye.

8, 17, 26

If you were born on the eighth, seventeenth, or twenty-sixth of any month, the best protective stones for you are light blue aquamarine, labradorite, lapis lazuli, reddish-brown or gray opal, blue sapphire, and turquoise.

9, 18, 27

If you were born on the ninth, eighteenth, or twenty-seventh of any month, the best protective stones for you are amber, carnelian, red coral, garnet, red opal, and ruby. You might also choose a *navaratna* ring.

However, if the total of your month, day and year of birth reduce down to either 2 or 7, you should replace the red coral, garnet and ruby with cat's-eye, moonstone, pearl, and tiger's-eye.

Your Full Date of Birth

There are also lucky stones for your entire date of birth, reduced down to a single digit.

1. Ruby, yellow sapphire, topaz

2. Cat's-eye, moonstone, pearl, tiger's-eye

3. Amethyst

4. Golden-red garnet, blue sapphire, hessonite

5. Diamond

6. Emerald, peridot

7. Cat's-eye, moonstone, pearl, tiger's-eye

8. Lapis lazuli, blue sapphire

9. Coral

Navaratna Ring

Arguably the oldest Indian amulet is the *navaratna* ring (also known as Nav-Ratna), which is worn on the ring finger of the right hand. The word *navaratna* means nine gemstones. The back setting of the ring is kept open to enable all the rings to remain in contact with the skin.

The rings are arranged in three rows. Topaz, chrysoberyl (a type of cat's-eye), and emerald make up the first row. The second row contains sapphire, ruby, and garnet, and the third row hessonite, coral, and pearl. These gems correctly align all of the planetary forces, providing good luck and protection to the person who wears the ring.

The stones should be of the best quality that the person can afford. The better the quality of the stones, the greater and more powerful the protection.

Protective Stones

In addition to stones that relate specifically to your birth sign or day of birth, there are other stones that can be used because of their protective qualities. Here are some of the more useful stones for protection.

Agate

The Romans believed that a wrestler who wore agate would be invincible. According to Marbodus, the eleventh-century bishop of Rennes, "the wearer of an agate shall be made agreeable and persuasive to man, and have the favor of God."[8] Because of this, merchants started wearing agate as a talisman and charm. In the fourteenth century, Chevalier Jean de Mandeville wrote that agate protected the wearer from snakebites, eliminated thirst, and protected the body.[9] Today, agate—especially blue lace agate—is worn to enhance communication skills and to eliminate nervousness. Moss agate is useful for protection, as it nurtures your inner strength and balances your emotions.

Amber

Amber has been used for protection purposes throughout history. Amulets and talismans made from amber have been found in Stone Age archaeological sites. Five bears, a bird, and an elk carved from amber dating back to approximately 7000 BCE were discovered in Bølling Lake, Denmark. They are the oldest three-dimensional works of art to be found in northern Europe. Other examples have been found in excavations of prehistoric sites at Indersoen, Norway. In Roman times, babies were adorned with amber bracelets to ward off evil spirits. Amber makes a powerful protective amulet that also attracts good people into your life. It is also said to bring the wearer closer to God. If possible, carry or wear an amber amulet that has been carved into the shape of a totem or favorite animal. Amber is available in colors ranging from pale yellow to green, to dark red and on to deep brown. Golden amber strengthens close relationships.

Amethyst

Amethyst is a healing stone that relieves tension, stress, and depression. As amethyst enhances psychic communication, it is useful for protection purposes and provides insights into situations you might find difficult to resolve using logic alone. A piece of amethyst placed under the pillow is believed to cure insomnia.

Aquamarine

Aquamarine promotes tolerance and understanding. It also helps people who feel overwhelmed by everything they have to do to stand up for themselves and say no when necessary.

Aventurine

Aventurine is considered a lucky stone that attracts both money and success. It is useful for protection purposes too, as it calms troubled emotions and encourages thought before action.

Beryl

Beryl has traditionally been carried or worn to provide protection when traveling over water. It also wards off evil spirits, and other forms of negativity.

Bloodstone

Bloodstone is a good stone for children to carry or wear, as it provides protection and ensures they remain healthy and hale.

Calcite

Calcite is a useful stone available in every color of the rainbow. Consequently, it is useful for balancing the chakras (see chapter 6). Calcite also provides protection for the chakras and encourages spirituality.

Carnelian

Carnelian provides the wearer with energy, confidence, and courage. It allows the person to stand up for him- or herself and speak boldly when required.

Cat's-eye

Not surprisingly, cat's-eye is used to avert the evil eye. It also protects the owner from witchcraft and evil spirits.

Chrysoprase

Chrysoprase is used for general protection purposes. It is also considered a money stone, and many people carry one with them to attract wealth.

Diamond

Diamond eliminates negativity and encourages a positive approach to life. It enhances close relationships and provides confidence to both people in the relationship. It attracts abundance in all ways and can also be used for all forms of protection.

Gypsum

Gypsum is worn or carried for protection, and it also attracts good luck. In Russia, yellow gypsum was cut into the shapes of eggs, which became fertility symbols.

Halite

Halite is solidified salt. It is used for both grounding and protection. Placing a halite crystal at each corner of your house will provide protection for everyone living there.

If someone is deliberately causing you problems, you can force them to stop by writing the person's name on a small piece of white paper. Fold the paper into a tiny square and place a halite crystal on top of it. This will not harm them in any way, but will force them to stop whatever it is they are doing to hurt you.[10]

Jade

Jade is worn to attract good luck. It is especially lucky for people with birth dates that reduce down to 2, 6, or 7. It helps people handle difficult situations, and is useful for protection purposes.

Red Jasper

Red jasper has traditionally been worn for protection purposes. It soothes anger and encourages friendship and harmony in the home.

Malachite

Malachite was considered a sacred stone by the ancient Egyptians. It enhances the immune system and is renowned for healing the mind, body, and spirit. People wear it for personal protection and for creative purposes. In the past, pregnant women wore it to protect their unborn babies.

Consequently, malachite came to be used to protect young children, and malachite was attached to the side of babies' cots to protect them from evil spirits.

Moonstone

Moonstone makes a useful protective amulet, as it encourages calmness and enables the wearer to remain in control of his or her emotions.

Obsidian

Black obsidian is the most popular stone for grounding purposes. It helps people return to reality and place their feet firmly on the ground. However, it should be used carefully, as it makes some people feel depressed.

Ruby

Ruby creates feelings of positivity and well-being. It is an important protective stone that is often worn to avert bad luck or misfortune.

Sugilite

Sugilite heals painful emotions and encourages forgiveness, both of self and others. It is worn or carried to provide protection from anger and negative thoughts.

Black Tourmaline

Black tourmaline is a strikingly beautiful stone of immense power. It is considered the most powerful of the black gems. It works by deflecting negative energy away from the person who is wearing it. It acts, therefore, as a powerful protective shield that repels all negativity and psychic attack, no matter where it comes from. Black tourmaline also helps people turn their hopes and dreams into reality.

Turquoise

In medieval Europe, turquoise was attached to the bridles of horses as an amulet to prevent them from illness, especially after a day of hard riding.

Native Americans in New Mexico and Arizona carve turquoise into animal shapes called fetishes, which are worn on a necklace as a protective amulet.

Fetishes were originally West African amulets, but nowadays they are considered to be more than that as they also contain spirits. Hunters also use them as talismans. A turquoise attached to a rifle will ensure an accurate shot.

Today, turquoise is worn for healing, protection, and insight.

How to Choose Protective Gemstones

Gemstones and crystals are readily available in larger cities where there are specialist stores that sell them. Many New Age stores also have a small range of gemstones for sale. It is not as easy for people living in smaller centers to obtain gemstones and crystals, but fortunately there are many suppliers offering them over the Internet.

Ideally, you should choose your gemstones and crystals yourself. I find it amazing that whenever I look at an array of a particular stone, one of them will somehow attract my attention, and that will be the one I buy. Frequently, I'll go to a crystal store intending to buy a certain stone, and end up buying several others as well, because they "spoke" to me.

I have different methods to help me find the right stone to buy. I'll hold the crystals one at a time, until one "feels" right. If I'm finding it hard to choose between two crystals, I'll place one to my left side and the other to my right. I'll close my eyes and relax for a few seconds, and then ask myself which stone would be more beneficial to me at this time. When I open my eyes, I'll find that I'm leaning toward the stone that I should buy. This is a form of dowsing known as body dowsing. The other method I use is to hold a pendulum over the stones I'm interested in and allow it to tell me which stones to buy.

You should never shop for crystals or gemstones if you are feeling angry or are in a rush. Allow plenty of time, so the crystals can "talk" to you. A friend of mine says she can hear the crystals singing to her. Several people I know feel a slight tingling sensation in their fingers when they're holding the stone that is right for them. You will miss these subtle energies if you try to buy crystals in a hurry or if you are harboring negative emotions.

Caring for Your Crystals and Gemstones

Although they feel hard and solid, crystals and gemstones can be scratched or chipped if they are not cared for properly. Wrap them individually when moving them from place to place. Instead of casually tossing your crystal into a pocket or purse, place it into a pouch or small bag first to protect it.

As your crystals pick up both positive and negative vibrations, it is important to cleanse them to remove any negativity that they may have picked up before coming into your possession. This is especially important when you buy a crystal, as you have no idea how many hands it has passed through or how much negativity it has absorbed on its way to you. You should also cleanse your crystals on a regular basis to remove any residual negativity they may have picked up.

Cleansing

If you belong to one of the fire signs (Aries, Leo, or Sagittarius), you can cleanse your crystals with candles. Place your crystal in the center of a ceramic dish and surround it with several small candles. Light the candles and leave the crystal until the candles have burned out. Another method is to quickly pass your crystal through the flame of a candle. However, you should never do this with an opal, as the flame is likely to damage it.

If you belong to one of the earth signs (Taurus, Virgo, or Capricorn), you can cleanse your crystals by burying them in earth for twenty-four hours. If you don't have a garden you can use a plant pot or some other container filled with soil. After twenty-four hours have passed, retrieve the crystals and wash them in pure water to remove any soil, and allow them to dry naturally.

If you belong to one of the air signs (Gemini, Libra, or Aquarius), you can cleanse your crystals with a smudge stick. Allow every part of your crystal to receive benefit by slowly moving it around in the smoke. Alternatively, you can use a smudging spray to cleanse your crystal.

If you belong to one of the water signs (Cancer, Scorpio, or Pisces), you should cleanse your crystals with water. The best source of water for this purpose is a natural one, such as a spring, stream, river, or waterfall. Hold your crystals under the water for a minute or two, and then allow them to dry naturally. If you do not have access to any of these, place your crystals in a bowl and pour bottled spring water over them. Leave them in the water for a few minutes and allow them to dry in the sunlight.

There are also many other ways to cleanse your crystals. You can bury them for twenty-four hours in a bowl of organic, uncooked brown rice. The rice will absorb all the negativity and should not be eaten.

If you own a large cluster of quartz crystal, you can cleanse your crystals by placing them on it for a few hours.

You can rest the crystal on the palm of your right hand, and rest the back of this hand on your left palm. Say a prayer, mantra, or positive affirmation over the crystal, and visualize the negativity disappearing and being replaced with positive energy.

How to Use Gemstones for Psychic Protection

There are many ways of using crystals and gemstones for psychic protection. You can place a crystal under your pillow to provide you with protection while you're asleep. You can place crystals in different rooms of your home to promote peace and harmony, as well as protection. A piece of quartz crystal placed in all four corners of a room will provide protection and create a harmonious environment. The points of the crystals should face the center of the room. Crystals that are used to protect rooms in this way should be cleansed every week.

If you place a piece of purple fluorite close to your computer and television, it will protect you from the electromagnetic waves they emit.

If members of your household suffer from stress, anger, or frustrations, place a piece of amethyst or smoky quartz in the areas they most frequent. This will help to calm the stressed person and will protect other family members from any negativity the stressed individual creates.

Meditate with your crystals to gain healing as well as a sense of tranquility, harmony, and inner peace.

How to Wear Your Gemstones

You can wear your protective stones in any way you wish. They can be set into rings or made into tie-pins, bracelets, necklaces, earrings, or other items of jewelry. Alternatively, you might like to carry them in a small bag in your wallet or purse.

Use your intuition to tell you exactly where you should wear them. You may not consciously know where your body craves the energy that the gemstone can provide, but almost invariably you'll choose the correct position if you follow your intuition.

One wonderful aspect of wearing gemstones for psychic protection is that you can wear them openly, as most people will consider them decorative adornments and have no idea of your real reasons for wearing them.

Salt

I have saved salt, the most important crystal of all for psychic protection, to finish this chapter.

The ancient Egyptians, Greeks, and Romans made offerings of salt and water to their gods. This indicated its importance and made it a worthy offering to the divine source of all life.

Salt is essential for life. It regulates blood pressure, helps carry nutrients to the cells of the body, and ensures the optimal growth of fat, bone, and muscle tissues. A deficiency of salt creates fatigue, loss of motivation, and feelings of depression.

The importance of salt is reflected in many common phrases, such as "he's the salt of the earth," and "I'll take that with a grain of salt." In the Sermon on the Mount, Jesus called his followers "the salt of the earth" (Matthew 5:13). St. Paul wrote: "Let your speech be always with grace, seasoned with salt, that ye may know how ye ought to answer every man" (Colossians 4:6). Middle Eastern people have a saying, "There is salt between us," indicating a close relationship between two people. The Persian phrase "untrue to salt" refers to someone who is disloyal.

The word *salary* comes from the Latin word *sal*, which means salt. Although it is not true, many people believe Roman soldiers were paid in salt. In actuality, the soldiers were given an allowance of salt. Later, in imperial times, they were given an allowance of money for salt. The word *salad* also comes from *sal*, as the Romans salted their leafy vegetables.

Salt has also been used for purification purposes. Salt is incorruptible and is used to preserve other food to prevent decay. For thousands of years, it has been used to provide protection from the forces of evil. A pinch of salt in a cradle would protect a baby until it was baptized. If a plate of salt was brought to the christening by the parents and kept close to the baby during the service, he or she would be assured of ultimately going to heaven. In the English Midlands, oaths could be taken on salt instead of the Bible. Prayers made near salt would always be answered.[11]

Naturally, there are many superstitions associated with salt. It is considered bad luck to spill salt. In Yorkshire, until the end of the nineteenth century, people believed that someone in the family would shed a tear for every single grain of salt that was spilt. The remedy was to throw a small amount of salt over your left shoulder.

People believed salt would protect them from evil spirits, as the spirits would have to count each grain of salt before harming the occupants of the house. As this was such an arduous task, the evil spirits would give up and go elsewhere.

Salt can be sprinkled in the four corners of a room to provide protection. It can also be added to baths to protect the person bathing and to ward off evil.

Now that we've covered the most effective methods of psychic protection, we'll start learning how to use them.

five

How to Protect Yourself

Before you can protect others, you must be able to protect yourself. This is similar to the words used by flight attendants when they tell you if there's an emergency, to put on your own breathing mask before putting one on a child in your care. Obviously, you're not going to be able to help others very much if you're experiencing some form of psychic attack and are unprotected yourself.

Someone who is well grounded, has a positive approach to life, and feels good about him- or herself is naturally protected. Someone who is timid, fearful, and full of worries is open to any and every form of negativity. This person may even be attacked by his or her own negative thoughts. Most people fall somewhere between these two extremes. Consequently, for most people there will be times when they need psychic protection of one sort or another, but most of the time they will have enough natural protection to help them progress in everyday life.

There are a number of ways you can strengthen yourself to make yourself impervious to psychic attack:

- You can ground yourself
- You can change your attitude
- You can strengthen your aura
- You can control your emotions
- You can work on your physical body
- You can wear an amulet or charm
- You can use scents and perfumes
- You can develop your intuition

How to Ground Yourself

Grounding yourself ensures that you return safely to your everyday life after performing a meditation, a visualization, or some other form of psychic work. It is important to do this after spiritual practice, too. Sometimes people experience a sense of being spaced-out and not in control after exercises of this sort. If you feel distracted, unfocused, light-headed, or dizzy, you should ground yourself as quickly as possible.

At its most basic, grounding yourself can be accomplished by eating a snack, sipping water, stretching, stamping your feet, washing the dishes, or performing some other mundane, everyday task. These activities all help you focus on the physical, rather than the mystical, side of life. If possible, ground yourself outdoors, as this allows the negativity to drain into the earth. Stamp your feet, jump up and down, or do a few push-ups to ensure all the negativity is released. After doing this, eat a light snack, even if it's just a handful of nuts and raisins.

By grounding yourself, you allow any negativity you may still be holding to dissipate and disappear. Consequently, you should consciously ground yourself on a regular basis. As grounding yourself eliminates negativity, you can also use it to get rid of negative emotions, such as anger. Gardening is a particularly good way to ground yourself, as it is calming, physical, and involves contact with earth. As a byproduct, you'll also be doing something to enhance and beautify your home.

Attitude

Your attitude is your state of mind. People who are naturally positive are less prone to psychic attack than people who have a more negative approach to life. While everyone experiences ups and downs at times, naturally positive people recover from these down periods more quickly, and consequently are "up" much more than they are "down." These are the people who see the glass as being half full, rather than half empty.

Self-talk, the constant chatter going on inside everyone's head, has a major bearing on a person's attitude. It can be an interesting and revealing exercise to pay attention to your thoughts for a whole day, and deliberately turn any negative thoughts around. Each time you hear yourself saying "I can't do that," you need to immediately replace that negative thought with a positive one along the lines of "Of course I can." Everyone thinks negative thoughts at times, but when people think more negative thoughts than positive ones, they lose confidence and self-esteem, and can make themselves easy targets for psychic attack.

Another useful way to improve your attitude is to start looking for the good in others. You are more likely to experience the good when you expect it to occur. There is the saying that to receive love, you have to express love. In fact, the more love you give out, the more you will receive in return. Naturally, this works with hate, as well. If you express hate, you'll receive it in return. Like attracts like. Expressing love helps you maintain a positive attitude towards life. It also attracts other loving people into your life, which in turn makes you more loving. If you continually express love, you'll seldom need any form of psychic protection.

Your Aura

Your aura is an electromagnetic field that completely surrounds your body. It is roughly egg-shaped and extends eight to ten feet out from the physical body of a healthy person. Someone who is physically, emotionally, and spiritually fit will have a large and strong aura, which provides him or her with energy and protection. Conversely, someone who is unwell or suffering from stress will have a small, dull, and faint aura.

Slow, deep breathing will help your aura expand and gain strength. I like to visualize myself breathing in each of the colors of the rainbow, one at a time, and imagine the colors spreading to every cell of my body, before radiating out into my aura. This helps the aura expand and fills it with energy. If I don't have enough time to relax and breathe in each color, I'll take a slow, deep breath, inhaling as much air as possible, holding it for a few seconds, and finally exhaling slowly.

"Let your light so shine before men, that they may see your good works" (Matthew 5:16). These words of Jesus could describe the aura of a worthwhile person who is psychically protected.

Because the aura plays such an important role in psychic protection, we'll discuss it in greater depth in the next chapter.

Emotions

It is said that most people mature physically, some mature mentally, but only a few manage to mature emotionally. I saw a striking example of this about twenty years ago when I took one of my sons to hear an internationally known motivational speaker. I had heard the man speak before and was impressed with what he said and how he presented it. I thought it would be helpful for my teenage son to hear him as well. Everything went well until the man's overhead projector malfunctioned. After fiddling with it for a few minutes, the speaker lost his temper and screamed and yelled at the people who were promoting the event. To say I was stunned would be putting it mildly. I respected this man, had read his books, and had seen him before. I was amazed to see him performing so immaturely. This speaker has since written more books and paid several visits to my city, but I haven't read them and haven't gone back to hear him speak. When I think of him, all I remember is his bad temper and childish tantrum.

It's not easy to control your emotions. Emotion always overrules logic. If someone is overcome with fear, for instance, he or she finds it almost impossible to think logically. Consequently, although your positive emotions provide feelings of joy and well-being, your negative emotions undermine every aspect of your being and have a physical effect on your body. Positive emotions have an immediate beneficial effect on the body, but negative emotions can make you ill and miserable. You must learn to encourage your positive emotions and limit your negative emotions as much as possible.

Someone who is emotionally mature is able to dismiss negative emotions such as anger, hostility, jealousy, and resentment. This person is also able to encourage positive emotions such as forgiveness, friendship, generosity, love, and tolerance.

It can sometimes be hard to avoid the negative emotions of others. To protect yourself from these, make circles with your thumbs and index fingers and interlock them to create a circle of protection. If you are sitting down, crossing your arms and ankles also provides protection.

Physical Body

Your physical body is a precious vessel that carries you throughout this lifetime. It should be nurtured and looked after. Unfortunately, many people take their bodies for granted. They live on junk food, fail to exercise, and are surprised when they become ill.

Nurturing your body with regular exercise and a reasonable amount of good food pays off in many ways. Not only will you look and feel good about yourself, you'll have much more vitality and energy with which to enjoy life. You'll feel stronger and more confident, and this provides protection and resistance against illness and any form of negativity. In addition, your aura will expand, providing additional protection.

Amulets and Charms

The word *amulet* comes from the Latin *amuletum*, which means "an act which averts evil." Amulets are usually worn to provide protection from danger, but they can also ward off illness and ill fortune. The ancient Egyptians had four words that could be translated as "amulet." They are all derived from verbs that meant "to guard" or "to protect." Most Egyptians wore a protective amulet or a lucky charm to help them cope with the problems and stresses of everyday life. They even provided funerary amulets to help the deceased on his or her road from the underworld to heaven.

Amulets are still popular today. A large amount of jewelry, for instance, is created more for protection than adornment. Nowadays, some people wear St. Jude or St. Christopher medals for adornment, but many more wear them for protection. The cross has been considered sacred for thousands of years, well before Christianity began. Many people wear a cross to proclaim their Christian faith, but many also wear it as an amulet.

Lucky charms are worn to attract good luck and good fortune. Many people wear charm bracelets containing a dozen or more small charms on it. These charms include miniature animals, hands, hearts, four-leaf clovers, horseshoes and wishbones. Sometimes it is hard to tell the difference between an amulet and a charm, as charms are often worn to avert bad luck as well as to create good luck. The humble acorn is an example of an object that is both an amulet and a charm. It has been considered an amulet since druidic times, when the oak tree was venerated. It is used as an amulet when people place acorns on window ledges in their homes to protect the occupants of the house. It is also carried as a charm to attract good luck and a long life. Small silver acorns are often found on charm bracelets.

My grandmother used to tie knots in all her kitchen aprons to protect her and the food she was preparing. The origin of this practice is no longer known. However, knots have been used to discourage evil spirits for hundreds of years. This is why you sometimes see knotted fringes in churches. The fringe confuses the evil spirits, while the knots trap them and prevent them from causing mischief.

Strangely enough, the clerical collar is also derived from this belief. People thought that evil spirits could be caught by the knot in the priest's tie and cause problems during church services. This potential problem was rectified when the collar was turned around, making it impossible for priests to wear ties.[1]

The French philosopher Blaise Pascal (1623–1662) firmly believed in the protective power of amulets and always carried with him, sewn into the lining of his jacket, a sheet of paper containing a handwritten message that he had written after a distressing experience. This occurred when his horses took fright while pulling Pascal's carriage alongside the Seine River. The horses ran directly towards the river, but the reins broke just as they were about to pull Pascal's carriage over a precipice. The horses fell into the river, but Pascal and his wagon remained teetering on the edge.[2]

Scents and Perfumes

We all take our sense of smell for granted. We enjoy pleasant smells and quickly move away from unpleasant odors. Most of the time we are not aware that we are subliminally aware of many other odors as well. It may seem hard to accept, but we all have the ability to smell other people's emotions and state of mind. This enables us to instinctively respond to the people we come across in everyday life. Consequently, many of the hunches and feelings we experience may well be faint scents that we experience only at a subconscious level. This provides additional protection as it enables us to respond quickly to any situation that doesn't "smell" right.

In addition to this, we can consciously use scents and perfumes for protection purposes.

Developing Your Intuition

Even though some people claim they have no psychic ability whatsoever, everyone experiences hunches and feelings at times. Have you ever met someone and instinctively liked or disliked him or her? Have you ever been offered an opportunity that seemed attractive but felt wrong? Every time you have known something and had no rational explanation for it, you've used your intuition. You can use the heightened awareness provided by your intuition as a form of protection.

You can develop your intuition in everyday life by paying attention to, and acting on, your feelings. Start by becoming aware of the way your body feels in different situations. Pay more attention to the apparent rambling nature of your thoughts. As you do this, you'll find yourself becoming much more aware of the subtle energies that surround you all the time. You'll also find life will become smoother, easier, and less stressful, as your intuition will protect you everywhere you go.

You can also develop your intuition by experimenting with some form of divination, such as palmistry or the tarot. It is possible to read palms and cards without using your intuition, but the best readers use their intuition as well as their knowledge of the divination method in their readings.

Releasing Negativity

You can protect yourself from negativity in many different ways. You can focus on no more than one thought at a time. Consequently, when you feel nervous or afraid, that is all you can think about. When you deliberately change your thoughts by thinking of a suitable form of protection, you are ninety percent of the way there, as you will start thinking about the thoughts you choose to have, rather than whatever it is that is making you feel the way you do. Following are some of my favorite ways to release negativity.

Circle of Protection

I discovered the value of the circle of protection when I worked as a hypnotherapist. Many people came to me wanting help in controlling stress. One of the most effective methods I found was to have them imagine themselves surrounded by an invisible shield that protected them from stress. They could feel the stress coming at them, hitting the shield, and being deflected away, while they remained calm and relaxed inside. In fact, the more stress outside the shield, the calmer they would feel inside.

Whenever you find yourself in a negative situation, all you need do is imagine yourself surrounded by a clear, invisible shield. If you want, you can visualize the negativity hitting the shield and bouncing off, while you remain safe and protected inside. When I do this, I picture myself inside a large invisible bubble that completely surrounds me.

White Light

Many Spiritualist churches recommend that you imagine yourself surrounded by pure white light whenever you feel the need for protection. Some people visualize the white light coming downwards from heaven, while others imagine themselves in the middle of an invisible fog of white light. It makes no difference how you picture the white light, just as long as you can sense it and know you are protected. Although this white light is not part of your aura, it is frequently called a protective aura.

Favorite Angel

You can call on your guardian angel, or any other angel, for protection whenever you feel it is necessary. I have called on Archangel Michael on a number of occasions when I felt threatened or sensed danger. Each time, he gave me the necessary strength and courage to handle the situation.

Crystal Remedy

If you carry a crystal or gemstone around with you, you can touch or rub it whenever you experience negativity, either from inside or outside yourself. Fondle the crystal whenever you feel lacking in confidence, experience doubt or unworthiness, or experience uncertainty about a certain course of action. You can use any crystal or gemstone for protection purposes. However, you may prefer to use one that relates specifically to you. Chapter 4 includes suggestions on choosing the right crystal for you.

Thumb and Forefinger

Many actors conquer stage fright by rubbing the tips of their thumbs and forefingers together before walking onto the stage. This action helps them to relax and release the negative fears that cause stage fright to occur. You can use it to protect yourself whenever necessary. It can be done imperceptibly, even if your hands are in front of you. As you do it, you'll experience a lessening of tension and a feeling that all will be well.

Sign of the Cross

The cross is considered a Christian symbol, but it was used for protection purposes well before the rise of Christianity. The hieroglyphics of ancient Egypt, for instance, contain several types of cross, including an ankh, X, + and T. The four branches of the cross relate to the four cardinal directions, the four quarters of the world, the elements of fire, earth, air and water, and can even symbolize a crossroad where the paths of the living and dead cross. Consequently, the cross has always been considered a potent symbol that can be used for protection purposes.

You can trace a sign of the cross on your chest or abdomen whenever you feel the need for additional protection. The solar plexus, seat of the solar chakra, and the center of the chest, home of the heart chakra, are extremely potent places to trace a sign of the cross.

Crossing Your Arms and Legs

Most people cross their arms and/or legs instinctively when they find themselves in a potentially difficult or stressful situation. You can protect yourself at any time by crossing your arms and, if you're sitting down, your legs. Alternatively, instead of crossing your arms, you can rest your hands on your solar plexus, providing protection for your solar chakra. If you need additional protection, place a book over your stomach and hold it in place with your hands.

Crossing Your Fingers

Crossing the first and second fingers provides protection against all dangers. It is also used for protection against something that may or may not happen. If, for example, you hear that someone is suffering from the flu, you might cross your fingers and say to yourself, "I hope I don't catch it. Fingers crossed!"

Take a Shower

Water absorbs negative energy and aids purification. A useful way to protect yourself after experiencing negativity or a psychic attack is to enjoy a relaxing shower. Enjoy the sensations of the water as it revitalizes every part of your body. You might like to wash your hair at the same time to ensure the water goes everywhere. While you are in the shower, visualize the water removing and draining away all the negativity of the day. When you get out, rub yourself all over with a clean towel.

If you have experienced negativity and are unable to take a bath or shower, wash your hands with soap and water. As you do this, visualize all the negativity draining away down the sink.

Enjoy a Salt Bath

Salt is commonly used for protection purposes as it absorbs negative energy. A leisurely bath in salt water will remove all the negativity that has become attracted to you during the day.

Draw a bath and add two tablespoons of rock or sea salt. Stir the water to enable the salt to dissolve. While doing this, visualize the salt and water cleansing and purifying both your physical body and your aura. If possible, relax in the bath for about twenty minutes before getting out. Pull the plug, and as the salt and water drain away, thank them for removing all the negative energies that had been surrounding you.

Prayer

When you pray, you establish an instant connection with the Divine. This provides comfort and peace of mind, as well as protection. You can say any prayer you wish. It might be as simple as "God, please protect me." Alternatively, you might want to pray for hours on end. The Lord's Prayer and the twenty-third Psalm are the most popular Christian prayers that people recite when they pray for protection. Over the last two thousand years, people brought up in a Christian tradition have used both of these for protective purposes. Naturally, people brought up in other traditions can gain protection by saying prayers that relate to their beliefs. In addition to reciting memorized prayers, it is a good idea to tell the Divine what the problem is and why you are asking for protection.

six

How to Protect Your Aura

The human body is surrounded in all directions by an egg-shaped energy field called the aura. It is a protective ring that extends eight to ten feet outwards from the body, and reveals the person's physical, emotional, and spiritual state. People who are healthy in mind, body, and spirit possess strong, vibrant auras that provide protection, as well as the necessary energy to enable them achieve their goals. Highly spiritual people are said to have larger auras than less spiritual people. Buddha's aura was said to have extended for several miles.

The aura is constantly moving and changing. Lines of force and energy radiate in a crisscross manner throughout the aura reflecting the person's thoughts, feelings, health, and spirituality.

The aura consists of several layers, known as subtle bodies. The layer closest to the body is called the etheric double. It is an extremely fine, almost invisible layer that extends for between a quarter to half an inch all around the body. It appears to work as a battery that recharges itself while the person is asleep. The etheric double contracts during the day and expands at night. People who are able to see auras examine the etheric double as any health problems show up here first. Potential health problems, and even negative thoughts, show up in the etheric double.

When people first start seeing auras, the etheric double appears invisible, but as their aura awareness grows they see the etheric double as a grayish, shimmering layer of energy. The other layers of the aura surround the etheric double. Auras consist of a basic color that reveals the person's mental, emotional, and spiritual nature. Radiating through this basic color is a variety of different colors that reflect various aspects of the person's makeup.

Have you ever met a person who could "light up a room" by entering it? That person's radiant aura is responsible for capturing everyone's attention. In addition, everyone expresses their moods inside their auras. Terms such as "red with rage," and "green with envy" probably come from this, as people who can see auras can discern people's moods from the colors in their auras. These colors appear and disappear quickly, as the feelings come and go. However, constant negativity can affect the aura permanently, showing how important it is to think and act positively.

Our auras constantly react with the auras of others. When you spend time with someone you like, the two auras will mingle. The ultimate example of this is when two people are in love. In this instance, the two auras merge into one large, vibrant aura. The other extreme occurs when you are in the company of someone you do not like. When this happens, the two auras are repelled by each other. This explains why you can instantly dislike someone you have just met, even if there is no apparent reason for it. Your aura has reacted in this way to warn you to keep well away from the other person.

Consequently, someone who is constantly thinking negative thoughts will gradually repel everyone who comes into his or her life. This person's aura will adversely affect the auras of everyone he or she meets, and this person will become friendless and lonely.

Have you ever spent time in the company of someone and felt totally drained of energy when he or she left? This is a sign that the other person has enhanced his or her auric energy by draining your energy. These people are called psychic vampires. A few people deliberately steal energy from others, but most psychic vampires are not aware of their doing so. Try to limit the amount of time you spend with these people. This may not be easy, especially if you live or work with one. If you are unable to escape a psychic vampire, you must learn how to protect your aura.

Many sensitive people feel mentally and physically drained after spending a day in a busy city or attending a crowded concert or other event. Many people who commute to work in crowded buses and trains also feel drained at the end of the day. This means their auras have been depleted by the auras of all the people in their shared proximity throughout the day.

My father-in-law was a farmer. He looked forward to visiting us in the city, but after a couple of days he'd be desperate to return to his farm. City life depleted his aura; if he'd been forced to stay, he would probably have become ill.

People with strong auras are able to withstand any outside pressure, including psychic attacks, as their auras provide them with a natural form of psychic protection. Conversely, people with weak auras suffer from a lack of protection and are more likely to suffer from emotional problems, illnesses, lack of energy, and tiredness. They're also more likely to feel unsuccessful, with little or no control over their lives. Because they feel ineffective and worthless, this becomes their reality. Fortunately, this downward spiral can be reversed.

There are many reasons why someone's aura may be weak. Stress and overwork affect the aura. A negative outlook affects the entire person, including his or her aura. Smoking, drugs, and excess alcohol all deplete the aura. A poor diet and lack of exercise take their toll, too. Fortunately, all of these negative factors can be changed, and this has an immediate effect on the person's aura.

Although the aura surrounds the human body, it is also part of every cell of the body. Consequently, the aura is actually an extension of the body, rather than something that surrounds it.

All of the exercises in this chapter take time to master. However, the protective capabilities of the aura are so powerful that it is worth spending whatever time it takes to learn how to perform the exercises instantly, as soon as the need arises. When you reach this stage you will have immediate psychic protection whenever you need it.

How to Expand Your Aura

If necessary, you can temporarily increase the size of your aura to provide additional strength and protection. This is a useful skill, as whenever you feel stressed or experience any form of negativity you can immediately protect yourself by expanding your aura.

To do this, visualize your consciousness going down deeply into Mother Earth. Allow it to feel nurtured and protected by Mother Earth. When it feels ready, allow your consciousness to race upwards and back into your body, revitalizing every cell as it does so. Once your physical body is full of this energy, allow it to expand out and into your aura. This exercise enables your aura to grow to any size you wish.

Once you have done this, add a protective color to your aura. Green, blue, and white are all good choices for protection purposes.

The Chakras

Inside the aura, situated alongside the spinal column, are seven energy centers known as chakras. Each chakra represents one of the colors of the rainbow. *Chakra* is the Sanskrit word for wheel or disc, because they appear as whirling circles of energy.

The seven chakras are:

1. Root chakra, situated at the base of the spine. This chakra keeps you firmly grounded and provides feelings of security and comfort. The color is red.

2. Sacral chakra, situated at the level of the sacrum, about two inches below the navel. This chakra represents sexuality, creativity, and emotional balance. The color is orange.

3. Solar chakra, situated at the level of the solar plexus. The solar chakra provides feelings of warmth, happiness, personal power and self-worth. The color is yellow.

4. Heart chakra, situated in the center of the chest, in line with the heart. The heart chakra relates to unconditional love, sympathy, compassion, and understanding. The color is green.

5. Throat chakra, situated at the level of the throat. The throat chakra relates to communication and self-expression. The color is blue.

6. Brow chakra, situated at the level of the forehead, just above the eyebrows. The brow chakra relates to thought, understanding, intuition, and an awareness of our spiritual nature. The color is indigo.

7. Crown chakra, situated at the top of the head. The crown chakra relates to spirituality, enlightenment, the higher self, and the interconnectedness of all living things. The color is violet.

How to Ground Yourself

Ideally, we should feel fully grounded all the time. However, this is not always possible, especially if you are working with the energies created by the top four chakras. It is a good idea to ground yourself before meditating or performing any form of healing. Fortunately, it is a simple process that can be done in a matter of seconds.

Sit comfortably in a straight-backed chair. Your legs should make a right angle at the knees and your feet should rest flat on the floor. Take a deep breath and hold it for a few moments. As you exhale, push your feet firmly into the floor. Your thigh muscles will tighten and you'll sense a flow of energy into the area of your root chakra. Relax the pressure and take another deep breath, pushing down with your feet again as you exhale. Do this three or four times at least once a day. This will energize your root chakra and keep you fully grounded.

Revitalizing Individual Chakras

As you can see, each chakra plays a valuable role in keeping you whole and healthy. Whenever you feel you are lacking the energy of a particular chakra, you can take ten slow, deep breaths, and visualize yourself inhaling the color that relates to the specific chakra. Imagine colored air gathering in the area of the chakra, soothing and nourishing it, while at the same time replenishing it with an abundance of vital energy.

How to Use Your Chakras to Protect Yourself

This exercise uses the chakras to provide psychic protection. In effect, you seal yourself inside a bubble of pure white light.

Sit down comfortably, close your eyes, and take a few slow, deep breaths. In your mind's eye, visualize yourself as if you were standing several feet away. "See" yourself sitting in the chair, breathing slowly and deeply. Look at the area around your neck and head and see if you can detect your aura. If not, simply imagine that it is there.

Inhale deeply, and notice your aura expanding as you fill your body with air. See it decrease slightly as you exhale. Take a few more deep breaths and watch your aura increase and decrease in size with each breath.

When you feel ready, imagine that with the next inhalation, you'll breathe in the most beautiful red color you have ever seen. Watch your aura fill up with red and then sense it moving down into the area of your root chakra. Exhale slowly, noticing that the red color stays in the area of your root chakra.

Take another deep breath, noticing that this time you're inhaling the most beautiful orange color you've ever seen. Sense it slowly moving into the area of your sacral chakra.

Repeat this five more times, breathing in yellow, green, blue, indigo, and violet. Each time you inhale, watch the colors appearing in your aura and then moving into their correct chakras. In your mind's eye, you'll be able to see all the colors of the rainbow inside your aura.

Your chakras will be completely revitalized by the time you reach this stage. This, all by itself, provides feelings of well-being and protection. However, you are not finished yet. Take three more slow deep breaths, and then visualize a pure white light surrounding your aura. You'll notice it first as a slight, faint outline surrounding your aura but as you watch, you'll notice it becoming thicker and denser as it creates a layer of protective white light all around your aura. You can make this aura as thick as you wish.

If you feel the need for extra protection, you might make it twelve or eighteen inches thick. However, for normal purposes, six inches is usually plenty.

Once you have visualized the formation of the bubble of protective white light, take three slow, deep breaths, familiarize yourself with your surroundings, and open your eyes. Remain seated for thirty to sixty seconds before getting up. Once you have done this exercise, you'll feel totally protected and able to handle any situation with ease.

How to Eliminate Negativity with Your Chakras

This is a useful exercise to do at the end of the day when you are ready for bed. You will need seven swatches of material, one for each color of the rainbow. I was fortunate enough to find a set of silk handkerchiefs that included all the aura colors, and I use them solely for this exercise.

Before snuggling in between the sheets, lie on top of your bed and place the swatches of material directly on your body or on top of your nightclothes, on the chakra position that relates to each color. Close your eyes and think about the day you have just experienced. Start by thinking about all the good things that occurred. These do not need to be major events. Someone smiling at you as you walked past is a positive incident and you should include it. Think of as many things as possible that made you happy.

Once you have done that, think about the less positive aspects of your day. As you think about each one, allow your body to let you know which chakra was affected. You might experience a physical sensation, or maybe a sense of knowing, telling you which chakra it was. Think of the swatch of color lying over this chakra and allow the energies of the color to spread into your body. When you feel ready, dismiss that particular negative experience from your mind and think of the next one. Repeat this until you have dealt with all the negative experiences of the day.

Once you have done this, direct your attention to each chakra in turn, starting at the root chakra. Allow the red color from the swatch over your root chakra to fill the root chakra with energy. Repeat with all the chakras in turn. When you have done this, remove the swatches, get into bed, and allow yourself to fall asleep.

We all experience a certain amount of negativity as we go through life. It is healing to release all this accumulated baggage before going to sleep. This exercise eliminates the baggage, and also provides another benefit, as it recharges the chakras at the same time.

Your Sacred Breath

You can use breathing exercises to strengthen your aura. If you sit quietly in a meditative state and take slow, deep breaths in through your nose, breathing in to the count of three, holding it for the count of three, and exhaling to the count of three, you will energize and stimulate your aura, making it larger and better able to protect you.

You can also imagine yourself breathing in each color of the rainbow in turn. This enables you to enjoy a rainbow meditation and energize your chakras at the same time.

If you feel depleted in any of the areas indicated by the chakras, you can breathe in whatever colors you need to revitalize them. If you are feeling lacking in confidence, for instance, you should breathe in several deep breaths of red energy. If you doubt your self-worth, you should absorb several deep breaths of yellow.

You can also send this energy to other people in your family. If someone in the family is grieving or feeling sad, take deep breaths while imagining them surrounded in a protective shield of green. If he or she is physically depleted, imagine the person surrounded with orange energy. Continue doing this on a regular basis until the problem has been resolved.

Let Your Aura Smile

This exercise enables you to revitalize your aura as well as your physical body. Sit down comfortably, close your eyes, and take three or four slow, deep breaths, holding each breath for a few moments before exhaling slowly.

When you feel pleasantly relaxed, forget about your breathing and smile. Allow the smile to spread throughout your face, and allow this feeling of happiness and well-being to spread throughout your entire body. Take your time and enjoy the feeling of smiling throughout your entire body.

Once your entire physical body is smiling, allow the smile to spread out into your aura. Visualize yourself inside a huge smile that encompasses your entire aura and physical body.

Enjoy the sensation for as long as you can. If you wish, you can expand your smile even more and send it to people you care about. You can send it to everyone in your home, city, country, or even the whole world, if you wish to.

When you are ready to continue with your day, focus on your breathing again. Take three or four slow, deep breaths and open your eyes.

After this exercise you'll feel totally rejuvenated in mind, body, and spirit. Your aura will have expanded and you'll feel positive about every aspect of your life.

With practice, you'll be able to do this exercise instantly, whenever you wish. All you need do is smile and allow your smile to infiltrate every cell of your body before spreading out into your aura, and then on to wherever you wish. This is a useful exercise to do when meeting people. Allow your smile to encompass the person you are meeting. This person's aura will respond favorably as a result, and he or she will sense your love and friendship.

How to Protect Your Aura

There are many ways to protect your aura. You can visualize yourself surrounded by a clear plastic shield. If you are in the company of a psychic vampire, visualizing a clear screen of glass or plastic will be enough to prevent him or her from draining your energy.

In more general situations, you might like to imagine that you are wearing a protective cloak that covers you from the top of your head to the tips of your toes. This cloak might be blue or green on the inside, but have a reflective substance on the outside to deflect negativity, no matter where it comes from.

Another method is to take several deep breaths. Each time you exhale, imagine yourself inside a clear protective bubble. Each exhalation expands the bubble until it is a comfortable size for you. If you wish, you can also request that this protective bubble stay with you for a certain period of time. Once that time period is up, you can renew the bubble if it is still necessary.

If you are about to face a difficult or challenging situation, you can ground yourself to the earth. You do this by placing both feet flat on the ground or floor, and imagining yourself rooted to the ground. Imagine you have strong roots that are planted deep into the earth. Take a slow, deep breath and as you exhale imagine this energy passing through all of your chakras from the top of your head all the way down to your root chakra and into the ground through your imaginary roots. Take another deep breath, and this time visualize the energy starting in the roots and spreading up through your chakras to the top of your head and out into the universe. Repeat this three or four times, and you'll find you can easily deal with situations that you would have found difficult and stressful in the past.

How to Strengthen Your Aura

Ideally, your aura should be strong enough to withstand most psychic attacks. However, you are exposed to huge amounts of negativity on a daily basis and this tends to wear down your aura. Most of the news you see, hear, or read about on television, radio, and newspapers is negative. Good news doesn't sell as well as bad news. You are also likely to pick up negativity from the attitudes and thoughts of the people you meet on a daily basis. Your own negative thoughts also affect the well-being of your aura.

Most of the time, your aura will be able to withstand these unintentional attacks. However, if you are feeling tired or unwell, your energy body becomes weakened and you will need to take steps to recharge and reenergize your aura.

Perform some breathing exercises to provide immediate strength to your aura. You will need to allow yourself approximately thirty minutes to sit down comfortably on your own, and think about everything you love. Send out thoughts of love to everyone you care about. Once you have done that, silently express your love to everything else you love. This might include places, possessions, pets, talents, and skills. Express your love to the people you dislike. Finally, express your love to all humanity. Finish by saying a few words of thanks to the architect of the universe.

Sending out love in this way strengthens, rebalances, and harmonizes your aura. A friend of mine who suffers from constant pain caused by an accident twenty years ago told me that he is free of pain for hours at a time after doing this exercise. Not surprisingly, he performs this exercise regularly, and every aspect of his life has improved as a result. Because he's constantly expressing love everywhere he goes, he receives an abundance of love in return.

How to Cleanse Your Aura

You should cleanse your aura whenever you have been exposed to negativity of any sort. Malicious gossip is a good example. Aura cleansing is a simple process than you can complete in less than a minute.

Rub your hands together vigorously until you feel them tingle. Starting at the top of your head (the crown chakra), clean your aura by sweeping your hands down your body. Start with your head and neck, and then clean your arms, chest and stomach, back, and finally, your legs and feet. At the end of each stroke, flick your hands to eliminate the negativity. To finish the process, stroke the front of your entire body in a long sweeping motion. Repeat with your back. Shake your hands vigorously when you've finished. If possible, wash your hands in flowing water. If you wish, you can perform this exercise with your fingers making contact with your skin. Alternatively, you can stroke the aura with your fingers a few inches away from the body. This is a matter of personal preference, and the end results will be the same. You should feel cleansed, refreshed, and invigorated after cleansing your aura.

Colors for Protection

The colors you wear provide emotional support and can be deliberately chosen for protection purposes. The material of the garment acts as a color filter that allows a certain color or colors to reach the skin where it can be absorbed by the body. Blue material, for instance, is blue because it absorbs all the wavelengths other than blue. Consequently, when natural light passes through it, it picks up the blue vibration, which can then be absorbed by the body. White material allows every color to pass through it, providing a veritable rainbow of color for the body. This is why white is a nourishing and purifying color that cleanses the whole body. It is a good color for protection.

Black is sometimes used for protection, too, as it reflects light away from the body. However, it is not a good idea to do this often as black also attracts negative energy.

Red

Red is a good color to wear when you need to feel confident and successful. It creates drive, ambition, and a positive outlook on life.

However, you should not wear red when you are feeling apathetic, listless, or drained of energy. You should also avoid it when you are feeling angry or if you have high blood pressure.

You might also choose to carry a red stone with you. Fire agate, bloodstone, red calcite, carnelian, red garnet, rose quartz, and ruby are good examples. They will also strengthen your root chakra.

Pink

Pink is a good color to wear whenever you feel the need to nurture yourself. Pink enables you to love both yourself and others. It can, in fact, attract love into your life. It makes you sympathetic and understanding.

However, you should not wear pink if you feel overly dependant on others, or if others are relying too much on you.

You might also choose to carry a pink stone with you. Examples include kunzite, pink coral, pink sapphire, pink topaz, and pink tourmaline.

Orange

Orange is a good color to wear if you are feeling sad or depressed, as it creates feelings of joy and laughter. It also helps you release long-standing negative emotions.

However, you should not wear orange if you are feeling unwell, as it can make matters worse.

You might also choose to carry an orange stone with you. Examples include amber, orange calcite, carnelian, citrine, golden labradorite, and orange topaz. They will also strengthen your sacral chakra.

Yellow

Yellow is a good color to wear when you need to think or express yourself. It enhances confidence, communication, and energy.

However, you should not wear yellow if you are suffering from low self esteem or are being subjected to frequent criticism.

You might also choose to carry a yellow stone with you. Examples include amber, golden beryl, citrine, yellow jasper, yellow sapphire, tiger's-eye, and yellow tourmaline. They will also strengthen your solar chakra.

Green

Green is a good color to wear if you desire good health, happiness, and abundance. It enables you to help others, as it promotes sympathy and understanding.

However, you should not wear green if you are making important decisions and need to act quickly.

You might also choose to carry a green stone with you. Examples include green aventurine, green calcite, chrysoprase, emerald, green fluorite, jade, green jasper, malachite, green sapphire, green tourmaline, and green turquoise. They will also strengthen your heart chakra.

Blue

Blue has always been considered a powerful protective color. Travelers to countries around the Mediterranean can't help but notice how blue is used on doors, window shutters, and around windows. This is done to protect the homes and the people who live in them. Blue is a good color to wear if you are feeling mentally exhausted and need to relax. It helps you gain self-respect, understanding, and a sense of responsibility.

However, you should not wear blue if you are feeling nervous, agitated, or depressed.

You might also choose to carry a blue stone with you. Examples include blue lace agate, amazonite, aquamarine, azurite, blue calcite, blue chalcedony, blue fluorite, lapis lazuli, blue sapphire, blue tourmaline, and blue turquoise. They will also strengthen your throat chakra.

Purple

Purple is a good color to wear when you desire peace, calmness, and time for meditation and prayer. Purple enhances your intuition and releases stress and anxiety.

However, you should not wear violet if you are feeling overly sensitive or are being imposed upon by others.

You might also choose to carry a purple stone with you. Examples include amethyst, purple fluorite, rhodalite, sugilite, and violet spinel. They will also strengthen your crown chakra.

White

White is a good color to wear when you need to keep your feet firmly on the ground and think matters through.

However, you should not wear white when you are feeling isolated or lonely.

You might also choose to carry a white or clear stone with you. Examples include clear quartz, diamond, white onyx, and white topaz.

Black

Black is a good color to wear when you need to feel self-sufficient and in total control. It enables you to make up your own mind and not be swayed by the opinions of others.

However, you should not wear black when you are feeling low or are not being fully recognized by others. Black enhances feelings of solitude and should never been worn when you are feeling lonely or isolated.

You might also to choose to carry a black stone with you. Examples include hematite, black obsidian, black onyx, black opal, and black tourmaline. (Black tourmaline is not easy to find, as it's brittle and jewelers tend to avoid it. However, it's a highly protective stone and is also often used for grounding.)

Color Shield

When people think of shields, they usually think of knights of old, wielding a sword with one hand and holding a shield to protect them in the other. Shields have always been used for protection, and this includes psychic protection. Fortunately, you do not need to make an actual shield to obtain the benefits that a shield can provide. All you need do is choose colors that appeal to you and create an abstract picture using them. Think of your desire for protection while drawing it, as this imprints your desire into the picture.

Whenever you feel the need for strength or protection, look at your picture for a few seconds, and you'll immediately feel calm and protected.

It's a good idea to create a new shield for yourself every now and again, as the colors you choose may change from time to time depending on what is going on in your life.

Candle Burning for Psychic Protection

As you have seen, colors can be used to change your mood and provide emotional support. When a candle is lit, it slowly releases the vibrational energies determined by its color. Burning candles enables you to experience the beneficial effects provided by the colors of the candles in a variety of ways, providing balance and protection.

The easiest way to gain these benefits is to meditate in front of a candle. Light the candle, sit down comfortably in front of it, and take slow deep breaths, inhaling the energy released by the candle. It is extremely relaxing to gaze into a candle flame knowing you're receiving the balance and protection that you're seeking.

You can choose the color of the candle using logic or intuition. You may deliberately choose a color that you feel will be helpful to you. Alternatively, you might randomly choose a color from a selection of different colors, trusting that the color you choose will be the right color for you at this moment. If you find it difficult to choose a color, burn a white candle, as it includes the entire spectrum of colors. White is a highly protective color that also provides calmness, peace of mind, and acceptance.

Types of Candles

Certain candles have been used traditionally for protection purposes.

Cat Candles

White candles in the shape of a cat are burned to provide protection for pregnant women. Black cat candles are burned to increase the potency of any magical ritual. White and black cat candles can be burned together, as they enhance each other's power, providing powerful protection.

Cross Candles

Cross candles, in the shape of a crucifix, are burned to provide general protection. Usually seven candles are burned, one each day for a week. The color of the candle is determined by the day of the week:

Monday: White

Tuesday: Red

Wednesday: Orange

Thursday: Blue

Friday: Green

Saturday: Black

Sunday: Yellow

Knob Candles

Knob candles, sometimes known as wish candles, are made from seven balls of wax with a single wick. One knob is burned every day for seven days. While the candle is burning, the person has to focus on his or her goal or wish. Knob candles can be obtained in a variety of colors, depending on the goal. White knob candles are burned to provide protection for you and your loved ones.

Novena Candles

Novena candles are cylindrical candles, enclosed in heat-resistant glass. They are usually burned for seven days, though you can also buy twelve-day novena candles. Novena candles can be purchased at religious supply stores. The best ones to use for protection purposes are novena candles with a picture of a saint on the front of the glass container.

How to Prepare Your Candles

When you are burning candles for protection purposes you need to clean and purify them to eliminate any negativity they may have absorbed while on their way to you. The most important part of this process is to dress or anoint your candles with oil.

You can obtain commercially made oils from specialty candle and occult stores. Nowadays, you can also buy them over the Internet. Some suppliers offer several hundred different oils, blended for different purposes. Despite this, most of the time I use baby oil that I buy at my local supermarket. This works well and is suitable for most purposes. If you buy commercially made oil, make sure that it is colorless, so you can use it on candles of any color. Colored oils can be used only on candles that are the same color as the oil.

Hundreds of different oils are manufactured for protection purposes. Saint Michael oil is a good choice for protecting yourself, and your loved ones. If you are burning candles to protect yourself from a psychic attack, I recommend Spiritual Protection oil, Ultimate Security oil, and Jasmine oil.

You should bless any commercially made oil you buy before using it. You do this by facing east and holding the container of oil as high as you can with both hands. Say out loud: "I bless this oil and consecrate it for the protection of my home, family, and loved ones. My purpose is good, and I ask for divine protection on this oil, my goal, and me. Thank you."

Cleansing Your Candle

This is the first stage of preparing your candle. Examine your candle carefully to make sure it is as perfect as possible. You might need to scrape off small imperfections or trim away any wax drippings. You might also like to wipe the candle with a tissue soaked in rubbing alcohol to remove any negativity the candle might be carrying. Rub from the base of the candle, up to the top, to draw all the negative energies out of the candle. Allow the candle to dry naturally. Once it is dry, you might like to buff the candle with a polishing cloth to give it an attractive sheen.

Dressing Your Candle

As dressing your candles can be a messy business, it is a good idea to wear old clothes, and to work on a surface that can be easily cleaned afterward. I like to dress several candles at the same time, as this means I have to clean up only once instead of several times.

Start by rubbing protection oil onto both of your hands. Hold the candle near the center, and starting from the center rub the oil toward the top of the candle. While doing this, think of your purpose in dressing the candle. As you dress it, you imprint your thoughts into the candle, and consecrate it for a specific purpose, which in this instance is to protect you and your family.

Once the top half of the candle has been dressed, oil the bottom half in the same way, rubbing from the center downward to the base.

There is a tradition that says if you are burning candles to bring something good into your life, such as psychic protection, you should rub from the top of the candle down to the base. Conversely, if you wish to eliminate something negative from your life, such as a psychic attack, you should rub the candle from the base to the top. This is personal preference, and you might like to experiment and choose the method that works best for you.

Some people have a strong aversion to oil. If you are one of these, you can dress your candle with water. You can use the same method that is used for oil, or you might use a spray bottle and cover the candle with a mist of water.

Winding the Candle

This is the final stage of preparing your candle. Hold your cleansed and dressed candle and think about how you are going to burn it to provide protection. While continuing to think along these lines, wind a thin ribbon around the candle starting at the bottom and finishing at the top. This binds your intention to the candle.

Your candle is now ready for use.

Candle Protection Ritual

For this ritual you will need to choose a candle to represent you. It can be any color you wish. You will also need either four or eight white candles that are noticeably shorter than the candle that symbolizes you.

Ideally, you should perform this ritual at an altar or sacred space in your home. If you do not have a sacred space, a small coffee or side table will work well.

Place the candle that represents you in the center of your altar, and surround it with the smaller white candles. Light the candle that symbolizes you, followed by the other candles. Light these in a clockwise direction, starting with the candle that is closest to facing north.

Sit down a few feet away from the candles and gaze at the candle that represents you. Notice how it is shielded and protected by the other candles. Visualize yourself surrounded by divine white light, in exactly the same way that the white candles are surrounding the central candle that represents you.

When you feel totally surrounded by white light, ask for divine protection. If you come from a Christian tradition, you might like to say a prayer, such as the Lord's Prayer. Pause for several seconds, and then say something along the lines of: "I need divine protection at this time, and ask (whichever deity you choose) to strengthen, guide, and protect me for as long as necessary." If you require a specific form of protection, tell your deity exactly what the problem is. Pause every now and again, to see what responses come into your mind.

Once you have finished your conversation, snuff out the candles, again starting from the north and going around in a clockwise direction. As you snuff each candle out, whisper thank you. Finally, pick up the candle that represents you. Hold it up as high as you can, while offering a sincere thank you to your deity for providing you with protection. Snuff out the candle, and keep it in a safe place. As this candle represents you, you do not want anyone else to handle it.

Another candle ritual, to provide protection from a specific person, is included in chapter 13.

In the last two chapters, we've covered a variety of ways to protect yourself. Now that you know how to protect yourself, it's time to learn how to protect others. We'll start in the next chapter.

seven

How to Protect Other People

Every now and again, you may need to protect others, especially your family and close friends. The most effective way of doing this is to help them to ground themselves. It's important that you're fully grounded before trying to help anyone else.

If the person you are protecting is conscious, and willing to receive your help, ask him or her to visualize a cloud of white light descending from above until he or she is totally surrounded with divine protection. If necessary, ask the person to suspend disbelief and simply imagine the cloud of white light.

Once he or she has successfully visualized the white light, take the person outdoors to make contact with the earth. This can be done through either the feet or the hands. Ask the person to visualize all the negativity draining out of his or her body through the hands or feet. Have the person visualize this for as long as possible. After this, give him or her a drink of water and something to eat.

After grounding someone else, you should ground yourself again too, as you may have accidentally picked up some of the negative energy the other person released.

If the person is asleep, you will need to do the visualization yourself. Picture the person completely surrounded by a protective white light, and then sprinkle a few grains of salt on the pillow above the person's head, below his or her feet, and on each side.

If the situation is such that you need to protect several people you can smudge them all, and ask them to imagine the smoke carrying away all of the negativity. If you need instant protection for a group of people, visualize white light descending over everyone.

You can also provide protection for a group of people ahead of time by cleansing and purifying the space they will be using.

Many years ago, I belonged to a spiritual development group. We took turns to meet in each other's homes. Whenever it was my turn to host the group, I smudged the room we were going to occupy an hour before they arrived. People commented on the pleasant atmosphere in the room, but even though I told them what I had done and why I had done it, none of the other members chose to follow suit. I'm convinced this was one of the main reasons why the group failed to survive. Providing protection ahead of time eliminates petty arguments, power struggles, ego trips, and other problems, and frees up the meeting for its intended purpose.

I used smudging to purify and psychically protect the room. However, other methods work just as well. Crystals, the sprinkling of salt, and prayer work just as well. When I was in South Africa I watched someone cleanse a room with a Tibetan bowl. The sound the bowl produced purified and protected the room instantly, creating a pleasant, harmonious, and safe environment for everyone in the room.

How to Protect People Who Are Away from Home

It is not necessary to be in the same room, or even country, as the person or people you want to protect. When I worked as a stage hypnotist, I was sometimes away from home for weeks on end. At least once a day, I sent thoughts of love and protection to my family at home. As the process is quick and easy to do, you can send protection to your children at school, your partner at work, or anyone else who you feel would benefit from it.

This protection ritual has seven parts:

1. Take several slow, deep breaths. This helps you to relax and focus on the ritual.

2. Close your eyes for about thirty seconds, and visualize the person you are sending protection to. As everyone "sees" things in different ways, do not worry if you can't get a clear visual picture in your mind. Some people can see the person as if he or she was in the room with them. Others get a sense or feeling of the person, without necessarily receiving any visual image.

3. If you are doing this ritual at your desk at work, open your eyes. If you are conducting the ritual privately, keep your eyes closed. Take three slow, deep breaths, inhaling as much oxygen as possible with each breath. Hold the breath for a few seconds before each exhalation.

4. Imagine yourself full of vital life force and energy, and mentally send it to the person you want to protect. If your eyes are still closed you might be able to sense the person

surrounded by a protective shield created by your breath.

5. Mentally send thoughts of love to the person you have just protected.

6. Take another three or four deep breaths to return to the present. If your eyes are still closed, become familiar with the setting you are in, and then open them.

7. Silently thank the architect of the universe for enabling you to send protection to your loved one(s), and carry on with your day.

This ritual also provides you with peace of mind, as you know you have done what you can to help someone close to you. On several occasions, people I have done this for have known about it at the exact moment I performed the ritual. On many occasions, people have contacted me to say they'd sensed my presence or had suddenly thought of me at the exact moment I was sending protection to them.

Aura Strengthening at a Distance

You can also use a similar ritual to remotely strengthen someone else's aura. Again, this ritual can be performed in a minute or less.

1. Take several slow, deep breaths to help you relax and focus on the ritual.

2. Close your eyes and visualize the person you wish to strengthen. It makes no difference how you visualize him or her, just as long as you feel a sense of psychic connection with the other person.

3. Once you have made this connection, visualize the person surrounded by his or her aura.

4. Focus on the aura and inhale slowly and deeply. Hold the breath for a few seconds, and exhale slowly. As you exhale, visualize the person's aura expanding.

5. Repeat stage four as many times as necessary until the aura is as large as you wish.

6. Send love to the person. Hold that thought for as long as you can.

7. Become familiar with the setting you are in. Take a few slow, deep breaths and open your eyes.

8. Thank the architect of the universe for enabling you to help your friend or loved one by expanding his or her aura.

Margot's Experience

At one of my psychic development classes Margot told us about an experience that changed her life.

"I was sitting at home checking my emails," she told us, "When I suddenly had a strange sense of foreboding. I knew it involved my son, Jared. He was twelve at the time, and he was playing with friends down the street. Actually, it was about half a mile away, but it was the same street. I didn't know what the problem might be, but I instantly closed my eyes and mentally surrounded him with white light. I then strengthened his aura. As soon as I'd done that, I phoned the house where Jared was. There was no answer, so I got in my car and drove there. There'd been an accident on the road outside the house. An elderly man had had a heart attack while driving his car, and the car had gone onto the sidewalk and hit a tree. The three boys had all been playing in the path of the car. The mother of the boys Jared was playing with was traumatized by what had happened, as the car had so narrowly missed the boys. She had been standing on the deck watching them play. Moments before the car went out of control, Jared had suggested they play soccer, and the three boys had turned to race to the back of the house when the car headed towards them. The mother had phoned for paramedics, and then collapsed as the shock of the narrow escape hit her.

"Later, I asked Jared why he'd suggested the change of game. He shrugged his shoulders. 'I don't know,' he told me. 'The thought suddenly popped into my mind.'

"To the best of my knowledge, Jared has never before or since suggested to his friends that they play soccer, so I'm convinced it was the protective shield that did it."

Children represent our future. Consequently, special measures have always been taken to protect the youngest and most vulnerable members of society. How to protect children is the subject of the next chapter.

How to Protect Your Children

The ceremony of baptism is one of the most common ways to protect children in the western world. In Christianity, the Devil is believed to be present inside everyone until it is forced out during the ceremony of baptism. Consequently, even today, some people believe that anyone who dies unbaptised will be claimed by Satan after his or her death. Unnamed babies do not fare well either, as they are doomed to roam the world until the day of Judgment.

Consequently, it was extremely important that babies were well protected until they were baptized and officially named. Garlic, salt, and amulets were used to provide suitable protection. An object made of iron was frequently attached to the cradle to provide protection, and an item of the father's clothing was often placed over the sleeping infant to provide even more protection. Babies were not taken out of their homes until the day they were christened. It was considered extremely unlucky, and potentially life-threatening to take an unprotected baby out of the home.

On the day of the christening, the baby had to be taken to the church by the most direct route. It is still considered good luck if the baby cries during his or her christening. This means that the devil has been expelled from his or her body. However, it was considered bad luck if the baby sneezed during the baptismal service.

Modern-day Christians usually wait until the baby is at least a few weeks old before christening him or her. However, in the past this would have been considered irresponsible and dangerous, as the child was in constant danger from demons, witches, fairies, and other potentially evil spirits until he or she was baptized into the Christian Church. The parents also had to keep the child's chosen name a secret, in case a witch somehow heard it and used it in a spell.

As well as placing the Lord's protection on the child, baptism was also thought to be good for the baby's health. Consequently, if an unbaptized baby fell ill, the parents would be just as likely to send for the vicar or priest as they would the doctor. As the holy water in the baptismal font was believed to have significant healing properties, many sick babies were hastily baptized in the belief that the holy water would cure them.

Young children are much more susceptible to psychic forces than adults. Most children are constantly picking up the thoughts, emotions, and feelings of the important adults in their lives. Because they are so attuned to what is going on, numerous methods have been devised to protect children from the evil eye and other forms of negativity.

In Bulgaria, a red thread is tied around the wrists of newborn babies to protect them and keep them safe. In Albania, young boys are often dressed as girls, as this confuses the jinn who consequently leave them alone. In southern China, young children wear caps in the form of flowers or animals, for the same purpose. Evil spirits think the children are flowers, owls, tigers, or other animals, and leave them alone.

Up until one hundred years ago, people believed that fairies could steal babies and leave a changeling (a fairy-child) in its place. In Devon, England, mothers pinned their babies' shawls to their dresses or the bedding in the cradle to prevent abduction by fairies.[1]

You can start protecting your children while they are still in the womb. Wearing red and blue clothing is helpful, as demons do not like these colors. A small piece of candy under the bed will protect the mother and her unborn child. This is particularly useful during labor, as the demons will be attracted to the candy and leave the mother and child alone.

Pregnant women should avoid cemeteries, as they are particularly susceptible to demons and other evil spirits that gather in graveyards. If you do inadvertently visit a graveyard, the remedy is to thoroughly wash your hands under running water as soon as possible after leaving the cemetery.

Certain gemstones can help women during childbirth. A necklace or ring containing jacinth or sardonyx was believed to help women during childbirth. Some accounts say that if the mother wears onyx she will give birth prematurely. However, the pain is lessened if an onyx stone is placed on or close to the woman during childbirth.

Lilith is a famous demon who was first mentioned in a ninth-century Hebrew book called the *Alphabet of Ben Sira*.[2] In this book, God created Lilith out of mud to be Adam's first wife. She was a determined feminist from the outset, and became annoyed when Adam insisted on always being on top when they made love. After many arguments about this, Lilith flew away to the Red Sea. God sent three angels, named Senoy, Sansenoy, and Semangelof to bring her back to Adam, but she refused. God told her that one hundred of her children would die every day until she returned. This did not work either, and Lilith swore that she'd harm all male babies less than eight days old, and all female babies less than twenty days old. However, she told the three angels that she wouldn't hurt any babies that were protected by an amulet that bore their names. As Lilith never returned to Adam, one hundred demons still die every day.

Consequently, an amulet that contains the names of the three angels, Senoy, Sansenoy, and Semangelof can be used to protect newborn babies, as well as their mothers. The amulet should be placed over the head of bed. Pregnant women should place amulets on four walls and the door of their bedroom. In Hebrew times, these amulets were written on parchment using ink that contained holy incense.[3]

Red ribbon and garlic placed on, or close to, a baby's cot also provides protection against demons.

Demons are said to hate metal. Consequently, a metal knife is sometimes placed under the pillow of heavily pregnant women to protect them and their unborn babies.

In his poem, *Charmes*, which appeared in *Hesper-ides* (1657), Robert Herrick (1591–1674) extols the virtues of holy bread as a way of keeping sleeping children safe:

> *Bring the Holy crust of bread,*
> *Lay it underneath the Head,*
> *'Tis a certain charm to keep*
> *Hags away while children sleep.*

Later in the collection, in a poem called *Another*, he recommends holy bread for adults, as well:

> *If ye fear to be affrighted*
> *When ye are by chance benighted,*
> *In your pocket for a trust*
> *Carry nothing but a Crust;*
> *For that Holy piece of Bread,*
> *Charms the Danger and the Dread.*

In England, before the Reformation, holy bread (bread that had been blessed by a priest) was distrib-uted to members of the congregation as a token of the love they should display to others. Bread baked on Good Friday was especially valued, as it protected the possessor from accidents and other disasters.[4]

Few people pause to wonder why blue is the color for boys, while pink is used for girls. Originally, young boys were dressed in blue to protect them from evil forces. Blue also protected them from witches, as it was commonly believed that witches hated blue, because it was the color of heaven. Children and livestock also wore blue beads to protect them from the evil eye. Even today, the front doors of many homes in the Middle East are painted blue to ward off demons and witches. Pink was adopted for girls relatively recently, as people felt it was unfair that girls did not have a color of their own.[5]

A good way to protect children is to take them to a store that sells crystals and gemstones, and allow them to choose one. Do not influence their choice in any way, as they will intuitively select the best protective stone for them. Tell the child that this is a "lucky" stone, and it should be kept in his or her bedroom. This stone will provide protection for the child while he or she is asleep.

A goodnight prayer is another effective way of protecting a child while he or she is sleeping. Although they may not be aware of the reason behind it, many Christian families also hang pictures of Jesus or angels in children's bedrooms. These provide protection, too.

Grace's Story

Grace is now ten years old. Six years ago, she and her family went away on vacation. In the garden of the house they rented was an old oak tree, and Grace was fascinated with the acorns that were liberally strewn all over the ground. When her father told her that people carried them as lucky charms, she filled her pockets with as many acorns as she could. By the end of the vacation, she knew that she needed only one acorn. She spent hours examining different acorns, and finally chose the one she intended to keep.

When the family returned home, Grace placed the acorn beside her bed, and it became her most cherished possession. Whenever she needed confidence or felt insecure, she would hold the acorn for a few minutes until she felt able to handle the situation. For a while, she carried the acorn around with her, but she stopped doing that when it occurred to her that she might lose it. Her parents offered to find her more acorns, just in case that happened, but Grace is insistent that her special acorn protects and helps her every day.

Children are highly vulnerable and need to be protected. Adults can also be vulnerable, especially when they're asleep. Consequently, a variety of methods have been devised to protect them during the nighttime hours. That is the subject of the next chapter.

nine

Protection During the Nighttime Hours

We are most vulnerable while asleep. Because of this, many fairy tales involve putting or keeping people asleep as the result of a magic spell. *Sleeping Beauty* is a good example of this. In this story, a beautiful young princess lay in an enchanted sleep for one hundred years until she was woken by the kiss of a prince.

There were also many spells that made the occupants of a house fall asleep so that robbers could help themselves to the family's possessions. In Scandinavian countries, a would-be thief could toss a human bone over the roof of the house he intended to rob, while saying: "As this bone waken, so may these people waken." As the bone could never wake up, this spell ensured that the occupants of the house remained soundly asleep until long after the thief had fled.

Variations of this spell were practiced in different parts of the world. In Java, to ensure the occupants remained asleep, thieves sprinkled earth taken from a grave all around the house they intended breaking in to. Peruvian Indian thieves placed charred human remains in front of victim's outside doors to ensure occupants would remain asleep.

The English *Observer* newspaper of January 16, 1831, reported an incident in which a group of thieves entered a house in the middle of the night, with a hand cut from the corpse of a hanged man. A lighted candle rested on the palm of this hand. The thieves believed that a candle in a dead man's hand would be invisible to the occupants of the house. The hand would also cause them to fall into a deep sleep, and remain in this state until someone put out the flame with milk.[1] It was a common belief in the past that a "hand of glory," as the hand cut from a dead man while he was still on the gallows was called, would enable its new owners to commit crimes without being caught.[2] The *Observer* account said that the spell did not work, as the thieves were discovered by the occupants and fled from the house, leaving the hand behind.

With thievery and spellcasting working together, it's little wonder people were concerned about protecting their homes while they slept. Nowadays, few believe that a magic spell might put them into a magical sleep, but are still aware that they need psychic protection during the nighttime hours. Fortunately, there are a number of methods that can be used to ensure you and the other members of your family can enjoy a peaceful and safe night's sleep.

Placement of the Bed

You should feel safe and secure while lying in bed. Feng shui, the ancient Chinese art of living in harmony with the world, places great emphasis on the placement of the furniture in the bedroom.

The best position for the bed is diagonally as far away as possible from the entrance to the room. The bed should be placed so you can easily see anyone entering the room, ideally without turning your head more than forty-five degrees. The bed should touch a wall to gain support. The head of the bed is considered the best side to be placed in contact with a wall. Ideally, the bed should be placed against a solid wall, rather than under a window.

The foot of the bed should not face the door. In feng shui, this is known as the "coffin" position. Chinese people used to be buried according to their horoscopes. This meant that sometimes bodies could not be buried until up to a month had passed. The coffins were lined up in front of temples waiting for the correct day to be buried. The foot of the bed pointing toward the door reminds people of this.

You should not be able to see yourself in a mirror while lying in bed. It is not good to have a mirror directly in front of the foot of the bed, either. If you happen to wake up in the middle of the night, and sit up, you might see your reflection in the mirror and receive a fright.

If you are trying to attract a partner, the bed should be accessible from both sides.[3]

There are three things you can do right away if you feel that someone is trying to psychically attack you while you are asleep:

1. You can change your usual sleeping time by going to bed earlier or later.

2. You can sleep in a different room for a few days.

3. You can temporarily change the position of your bed in the room.

None of these will resolve the problem on their own, but they will lessen the strength of the attack, and give you time to think about other ways to eliminate the problem.

Water

A glass of water placed at the head of your bed before you go to bed will absorb any negative energy around you while you sleep. This water is not for drinking. When you wake up in the morning toss out the water and wash the glass thoroughly, separately from any other dishes you may be washing. Once you have washed the glass, empty the sink and refill it before washing anything else.

Repeat this every night, and you will find that your sleep will become more restful and effective.

Salt

A pinch of salt placed under the sheets will protect whoever sleeps in the bed. Ideally, the salt should be sea salt or consecrated salt. Consecrated salt can be obtained from a Roman Catholic Church, or a store that sells Catholic religious supplies. Household salt can also be used, as long as you hold it in the palm of your hand for a few seconds and silently bless it before placing it in the bed.

Cedar Oil

Cedar is an essential oil that possesses powerful cleansing and protection properties. The cedar tree is considered a symbol of grandeur, strength, incorruptibility, and immortality. Because of these qualities, during the Middle Ages the cedar tree was associated with the Virgin Mary. Solomon's temple was constructed largely from cedar wood.

A drop or two of cedar oil in each corner of the bedroom will provide protection for everyone sleeping there. Cedar also encourages pleasant dreams. This makes it doubly useful for people who suffer from disturbing dreams and nightmares.

Prayer

Prayer is communication with the Divine, and many people pray before going to bed, or while lying in bed waiting for sleep. During your prayers you should ask for protection for yourself and your loved ones while you are asleep. This will enable you to fall asleep more easily, knowing that you, and the special people in your life, are surrounded with divine protection.

Prayer and salt make a useful remedy if you suffer from sexual dreams. Many people enjoy their sexual dreams, but people who are trying to develop spiritually sometimes consider them a hindrance and an unnecessary distraction. Praying immediately before falling asleep helps raise the soul to a higher level where sexual dreams do not occur.

Stephanie's Experience

My wife and I met Stephanie while traveling in Portugal. Stephanie was from Chicago and worked in the advertising industry. She was vacationing in Europe on her own, as she needed time out to recover from an unpleasant divorce. She was convinced that her former husband had tried to psychically attack her in her sleep.

"I started having nightmares. I'd wake up in the middle of the night trembling and shaking, and then find it impossible to get back to sleep," she told us. "After a week or so, this started affecting my work, as I was constantly exhausted. My kids suffered, too, as I became very short-tempered.

"A friend suggested I sleep in a different room. It seemed like a crazy idea, but I was prepared to try anything. To my surprise, I slept soundly in the guest bedroom. I had no nightmares, and slept all night long. After a couple of nights there, I thought the problem was over. I returned to my normal bed and, much to my surprise, started having nightmares again. I'm sure Grant was somehow attacking me in my bed, as when I returned to the guest room everything was fine. I slept in the guest room every night for a month. It might have been longer, 'cause I didn't want to experience the nightmares again. Eventually, I thought he must have given up by now, and went back to my old bed, and everything was fine. By that time he had a new woman in his life, and had stopped obsessing about me.

"Another time, maybe three months later, I was in New York on business. It had been a busy day and I went to bed early as I had a headache. Whenever I travel on business I always lie in bed and think about my kids until I go to sleep. This night, I somehow knew something was wrong with Jessica. It must have been my sixth sense, I guess. I called my mom to see if everything was okay, and she said the kids were fine. Jessica and Simon were missing me and looking forward to my return. We chatted for a while, and then I went back to bed. I still felt something was wrong. I remembered reading in a book about a bubble of protection, so I lay in bed and imagined a bubble of protection covering Jessica's bed. That didn't seem enough, so I made it big enough to cover the entire room. Then I thought of Simon. Surely, he'd need protection, too. And then I thought of Mom, who always slept in our home when I was away. So I made the bubble of protection big enough to cover the whole house. Funnily enough, I found it easy to fall asleep after doing that.

"When I woke up in the morning, I knew everything was all right. I phoned Mom and spoke to the kids. Jessica had fallen off her bike the previous afternoon. Fortunately, she hadn't broken anything, but she was badly bruised and shaken. I must have somehow picked up those vibrations, as I knew something was wrong.

"Now, whenever I'm away from home, I surround the whole house with a bubble to protect Mom and the kids during the night. I enjoy doing it, as it makes me feel close to them. It also makes me feel less guilty about being away from home."

Stephanie was effectively protecting her physical home, as well as her family. We'll look at other ways to protect the home in the next chapter.

How to Protect Your Home

People have always been concerned with protecting their homes and surroundings. Consequently, amulets, charms, and rituals were used extensively to ensure the safety of homes as well as the people living in them. Although many people consider these to be nothing more than simple superstitions, many of them are still practiced today.

In 1850, Mrs. Margaret Gatty, a vicar's wife, visited a cottage in Catterick, Yorkshire, and saw a "ponderous necklace" of holed stones hanging on the back of the door. The old lady who lived in the house was re-luctant to discuss the necklace, but finally admitted that it had been placed there to provide protection against the evil eye.[1] More than one hundred years later, in 1958, Juliette de Bairacli-Levy found two sets of holed stones in a cottage in the New Forest, England.[2] I'm certain that today, another fifty years on, people are still using them.

Many years ago, I saw a collection of charm-wands in the Strangers' Hall Museum in Norwich, England. These are rods, walking sticks, or rolling pins made from glass. In many of them, the glass contains a twisting pattern of varied colors. In others, the glass was filled with threads, beads, or small colored seeds. The theory behind charmwands is that any evil spirit would have to count the numbers of beads, seeds, threads or wavy lines before harming any object or person in the house. All negativity, including potentially dangerous diseases, was attracted to the charmwands, and could be removed by dusting the wands with a cloth every morning.

Witchballs, hollow balls filled with colored thread, serve the same function. They were usually made from green or blue glass and could be up to seven inches in diameter. It is highly likely that the ornamental balls on Christmas trees are derived from traditional witchballs. Apparently, they were placed on the Christmas tree to ward off the envious glances of visitors to the house who saw the abundance of gifts lying under the tree.

People who could not afford witchballs or charm-wands filled glass bottles with colored threads and placed them inside chimneys and above doors to provide protection. These are still occasionally uncovered today when English country houses are renovated.

Salt-filled glass rolling pins were also used to protect the home from witches and other evil spirits.

It is a simple matter to make your own witchball. The hardest part is finding a glass ball with an opening in it. You may find a suitable Christmas tree ornamental ball that you can turn into a witchball. You'll also need some spools of colored thread. You can fill the ball with red thread if you wish. I prefer to use mainly red thread, but also use small amounts of other colors. Finally, you'll need a few drops of frankincense or patchouli oil. If your ball is clear glass, you'll need to cover the inside with silver paint. You do this by pouring a small amount of silver paint, obtained from a hobby store, into the ball and rolling it around until the interior is completely covered with paint. Put it to one side until the paint has dried. Cut your thread into three-inch lengths and insert these into your ball until it is full. Do not force too much thread into the ball. It should be full, but the thread should not be compressed. Add a few drops of the oil, and finish by sealing the ball closed. You can hang your witch balls anywhere you wish inside your home. If you have made them from Christmas decorations they will look attractive hanging in a window, or as part of a decorative arrangement. (See also witch bottles in chapter 13.)

In the past, many buildings were protected by placing a human sacrifice in the foundations. Civilization had advanced by medieval times, and animals, usually cats, were used instead of a hapless human. From the fifteenth century until a hundred years ago, buildings were often protected with children's shoes and other footwear. These were usually single shoes. It is unusual to find a pair. Sometimes other items, such as purses and knives, are placed with the shoe.

This was not purely an English tradition. In the 1960s, a pair of woman's and boy's boots with the soles missing were found in the rafters of a house in Abbs Valley, Virginia. The footwear dates from between 1850 and 1860. In the 1940s, a child's boot dating from the mid-nineteenth century was found in the kitchen wall of a house near St. David's, Ontario.[3] This shoe can be seen in Lundy's Lane Historical Museum, Niagara Falls, Ontario.

If you happen to renovate an old house and find any object that was placed in a specific position for protection purposes, you should replace it carefully, as it will still be providing protection for the people living in the house today.

Every now and again, someone renovating an old house discovers something that had been placed in position centuries earlier to protect the house. In 1867, Edward Peacock of Brigg, Lincolnshire, renovated his house. About sixteen inches below his kitchen he found a pavement, possibly dating from medieval times. Some of the stones had been removed and replaced with fork heads, broken scythes and chains.[4]

Protecting your home starts before you move in. To attract all the good luck possible, tradition says the first things you should bring into your new home are a bucket of coal and a plate of salt. After that you should sweep the whole house using a new broom. Only after doing this should you bring your possessions inside and move in.

Housewarming customs have been practiced for hundreds of years to bring good luck into a new home. It means letting go of the past, and starting again in a new home, full of enthusiasm and positive energy. Housewarming presents also provide good luck to the family.

Mondays and Wednesdays are thought to be the best days on which to move house. The worst day is Friday. Buy a new broom when you move house. It is supposed to be bad luck to take an old broom into a new home.

When you first move in to your new home, you can bring good luck into the house by walking into every room holding a loaf of bread and a container of salt.

A housewarming party is an opportunity to show off your new home. Even more importantly, it brings good luck to the home and everyone who lives in it.

It is considered extremely fortunate to possess family heirlooms of any sort. They bring good luck to the home and the family, and at the same time demonstrate the importance of family traditions.

Blessing Your Home

It is a good idea to bless your home when you first move in. However, you can bless your home any time you wish, and I have met people who bless their homes on a regular basis. This is a highly effective ritual to perform a day or two before holding a housewarming party.

To perform this ritual, you'll need a hand bell for each person in the house, a dish of salt water for each person, some sprigs of rosemary, and a crystal for each room of the house. Any crystal can be used, but rose quartz is a peaceful yet strong crystal that will energize the whole home.

As the kitchen is traditionally considered the heart of the home, the ritual begins in this room. Before the ritual starts, choose a route through the house that includes every room and ends back in the kitchen again.

Start with a few moments of silence. Depending on your personal beliefs, you may follow this by saying a prayer or visualizing white light covering the entire house. The purpose of silence at the start is to emphasize the serious nature of the blessing. As the ritual itself is noisy and fun to perform, it's sometimes easy to forget the serious purpose behind it.

The head of the household then leads a procession through every room of the house. Everyone needs to ring his or her bell as vigorously as possible. Each room needs to be sprinkled with salt water. The head of the household pays special attention to the corners of the room, while the other members sprinkle around the doors, windows and walls. However, as it's difficult to continue ringing the bell and sprinkle water, some people will need to continue ringing their bells while others sprinkle water.

Once every room has received salt water, the head of the household leads the family through the house again, this time distributing sprigs of rosemary. Rosemary oil can be used if the plant is not available. This time, instead of using bells, the family can sing a chant or hymn as they move through the house.

The family goes through the house yet again, this time singing and placing a crystal in each room.

After this, it's time to go outside to bless the exterior of the house. This is done using the bells and salt water. Salt water is sprinkled all around the walls of the house, and then around the perimeter of the property.

To complete the ritual, the family returns to the kitchen, holds hands and gives thanks for their home and all the other blessings in their lives.

If desired, the house can also be smudged once the ritual is completed. The crystals and rosemary should remain where they were placed for twenty-four hours.

How to Remove Negativity from Your Home

Rooms, and even entire houses, can pick up negative vibrations. Animals are often more aware of these than people. When I was a teenager, my parents took the whole family to visit friends who managed a hostel for delinquent teenagers. The hostel was empty at the time, and we children had a wonderful time playing hide-and-seek with Bruce, our Labrador dog, in the huge building. It was one of Bruce's favorite games and the new setting made it even more fun than usual. Late in the day, my brother, sisters, and

I were hiding in a wardrobe in a small bedroom on the second floor. We could hear Bruce running along the wooden hallway and into the bedroom. Suddenly, he stopped and gave a blood-curdling howl, something we had never heard him do before. We could see Bruce through a crack in the doors. Bruce was facing away from us, his hair standing on end, looking at the far corner. He gave several slow growls and slowly backed out of the room. He raced downstairs to our parents and sat as close to my father as he could, with his tail between his legs.

We examined the corner of the room carefully but were unable to see or sense anything. Bruce was obviously picking up negativity that we were unable to detect.

My parents were enjoying afternoon tea with their friends and were probably not too pleased when the four of us raced in and excitedly told them what we had seen. The hostel manager was intrigued, as his cleaning lady had told him she felt strange whenever she was in that part of the building. Apparently, the former matron of the hostel had died in that room some years earlier, and Bruce was somehow able to sense her astral presence. The hostel manager told us he was going to have the room exorcised, and wanted us to bring Bruce back after it had been done. Unfortunately, he died shortly afterwards, and we never returned to see if the exorcism had released the negativity from the room.

You can use incense to rid your home of any negative vibrations. You will need self-igniting charcoal and dragon's blood, a mixture of various plant resins used in many incense blends. Both of these are readily available at herb or New Age stores. As you don't want to burn your house down, you'll also need a brazier or secure container on which the charcoal may be burned. I use an eighteen-inch square concrete block.

Start by opening all the windows in your home. Remove any family pets until you have finished the purification process. You might want to ask anyone who lives in the house with you to leave also. Purification rituals are best done on your own.

Place the concrete block on the floor in a central part of the house. Place the self-igniting charcoal in the center. Fill a large container with water and place it close by, just in case it is needed.

Light the top edge of the charcoal. Wait until the surface of the charcoal is red with heat, and then, using a teaspoon, gently place a quarter of a teaspoon of dragon's blood in the center of the charcoal. If you live in a large house, you may need to add an additional quarter teaspoon of dragon's blood. Wait until the first quarter spoonful has burned away before adding the second quarter spoonful.

Once the dragon's blood has burned away, wait for at least forty minutes before closing the windows.

The dragon's blood will eliminate all the negativity in your home. However, the ritual is not properly over until you have attracted good, positive energy to replace it.

The easiest way to do this is to burn frankincense. This is readily available from New Age stores and Catholic supply stores. A cheaper alternative is to use a church incense that contains frankincense. Wait for approximately an hour after eliminating the negativity with the dragon's blood. Replace the self-igniting charcoal, and light it. When it is red hot, add a quarter of a teaspoon of frankincense.

Single-Herb Incense

There are also a variety of one-herb incenses that can be burned on charcoal to provide protection. Bay, cedar, cinnamon, clove, copal, frankincense, juniper, myrrh and rosemary are all particularly useful for protection purposes.

Allspice is useful when you are entertaining visitors. It creates a harmonious environment and encourages pleasant conversations. It also attracts luck into the home. Allspice provides an additional benefit, as it helps resolve problems in close relationships.

Bay stimulates psychic perception. It is also used for healing, protection, and purification.

Benzoin is used for purification and prosperity. It also enhances the intellect. It is a useful incense to burn while praying.

Cedar is used for purification and to promote healing. It also provides protection and spirituality.

Cinnamon has a calming effect that dissipates anger and aggressiveness. It is highly protective.

Clove attracts love and money. It is also used for purification and protection.

Copal aids spirituality and intuition. It is also used for cleansing and protection.

Frankincense is useful for exorcism and protection. It also enhances friendship, love, and heart-to-heart communication.

Jasmine is useful for calming painful and emotional situations. It enables people to discuss matters in a calm and rational manner.

Juniper is used for exorcism and protection.

Myrrh is used for meditation, healing and protection. It is especially useful for people seeking peace of mind.

Rosemary is used for exorcism, healing and protection. It is also encourages a pleasant night's sleep.

Sandalwood provides feelings of calmness and serenity. It also enhances spirituality.

Incense Cones and Joss Sticks

Incense cones and joss sticks can be burned anywhere in the house to purify the area and to create feelings of positivity. A huge variety of these are available today. Experiment with the ones that seem interesting, and use them whenever you feel the need for help or protection.

The Protective Power of Iron

People have driven iron nails into the frames of doors for thousands of years. They did this to provide protection to the house or building. The origins of this were lost well before Pliny the Elder (23–79), the Roman scholar, mentioned the practice in his thirty-seven-volume encyclopedia, *Naturalis Historia*. Iron was the metal associated with Mars, the god of war. Mars was an enemy of Saturn, who ruled witches. Consequently, anything made from iron could be used to keep witches away.[5] Nails were driven into cradles and cots, as well as the beds of women about to give birth, for this reason. The best nails to use are rusty nails that have been found lying on the ground.

Iron has always been considered to have apotropaic properties, meaning iron has the power to ward off evil spirits and bad luck. Consequently, this makes iron a popular material for amulets and charms. Amulets made from meteoric iron were found in the tomb of Tutankhamun. Until recently, Egyptians would call out, "Iron, you devil!" before entering dark or potentially dangerous places. This drove away any malevolent spirits who might be lingering there.[6]

Many old graveyards are surrounded by iron fences, as these effectively ward off any evil spirits. Iron used to be placed into the cribs of newborn babies to protect them from fairies who might steal them and leave a changeling in its place.

Horseshoes have been hung over doors to protect the occupants of the house since at least the fifteenth century. Horseshoes combine both iron and the shape of the crescent moon to create a powerful amulet. The crescent moon is associated with the Moon Goddess, and provides protection against bad luck and the evil eye.

Good luck is attracted to the house if the horseshoe is fastened with the points facing upwards. However, the horseshoe provides protection for the occupants if the points face downwards. Horseshoes should always be attached to the house with an odd number of nails. It is considered especially fortunate if the horseshoe is nailed above the door using its own original nails.

Blacksmiths were at one time thought to possess supernatural powers, as they worked with iron and fire, two mysterious and powerful substances.

There's a charming English legend told about St. Dunstan (c. 909–988), who was a blacksmith before he entered the church, and ultimately became Archbishop of Canterbury. One day a strange figure wearing a cloak asked Dunstan to shoe him instead of his horse. Naturally, Dunstan was suspicious, especially as he knew Satan had cloven hooves. He pounded the nails into the devil's feet with such force that Satan screamed with pain. Before he left, Satan promised never to enter a house that was protected by a horseshoe over the door. A similar nursery rhyme tells another blacksmith-related tale:

> *St. Dunstan, as the story goes,*
> *Once pull'd the devil by the nose*
> *With red-hot tongs, which made him roar,*
> *That he was heard three miles or more.*

When I lived in Cornwall, England, my landlady kept iron knives under the doormats of her front and back doors. Her best friend kept scissors under her doormats. They did this to prevent evil spirits from entering their homes.

Floor Wash

You can wash the floor of your home with a protective floor wash whenever you wish. You do not need to wait until you feel it is necessary. A floor wash to protect your home and to repel negativity is done from the back of the house to the front. Finally, the water is washed out the front door. If your home has more than one level, start from the top level and work downwards.

Ideally, the wash should be done with rainwater, or water obtained from a spring or stream. If that is not possible, ordinary tap water will also work. However, as natural water is considered better because it is untreated, try to obtain it, if at all possible.

Add a teaspoon each of salt, garlic, and vinegar to a bucket of water, and use this for the wash. Dispose of any left over water outside and to the east of your front door.

Traditionally, washes were always done before sunrise, to eliminate the negativity before daylight arrived. However, they can be done whenever you feel the need for protection. A good time to do it is immediately after an unwanted or unpleasant visitor has left the house. This means he or she is unlikely to ever return.

If you purify your home with incense after a floor wash, you effectively use all four elements. Water comes from the water you use in the floor wash. The Earth element comes from the salt, garlic, and vinegar. Fire comes from the burning of the incense, and Air is the smoke created as a result.

How to Cleanse Your Home

Cleansing is the term used to describe the removal of negative energies from your home and work environments. Depending on the situation, you can do this in two different ways: you can remove the negative energy, or increase the level of positive energy.

You might remove the negative energy by placing garlic in every room of the house, and leaving it there overnight. Gather up the garlic in the morning and burn it outdoors.

You might choose to increase the positive energy by placing flowers with pleasing scents in every room. Roses are traditionally used for this, but any sweet-smelling flower will work well. Placing mint in each room also has the effect of eliminating negative energy, while at the same time increasing the amount of positive energy.

Salt has always been used to ward off negativity, and is useful for cleansing your home. Prepare a solution of sea salt and water. Silently bless it, and thank it for cleansing your home. Using your fingers, splash a few drops of the solution in every corner of the rooms you are cleansing. Finish by splashing a small amount in the center of each room. If you are cleansing your entire home, remember to cleanse the cellar, attic, and garage. The atmosphere of your home should feel different in less than twenty-four hours.

You can do any of these if you experience negativity in one room of the house. Alternatively, you might place a large crystal in the center of the room, and keep all the doors and windows closed for at least a week. The crystal will absorb all the negativity in the room. At the end of this time, bury the crystal in earth for two or three months to allow it to cleanse itself and eliminate the negativity it has absorbed.

Another useful method is to sit in the center of the room that needs cleansing. Close your eyes and visualize the room you are in as clearly as possible. People visualize in different ways. You might be able to clearly "see" the room in your mind. You might see it faintly, or not at all. You might sense the feel of the room, or even "hear" it in your mind. It makes no difference how you visualize the room. Once you have reached this state, visualize all the negativity moving towards a window or door. I imagine a giant vacuum cleaner sucking all the negativity towards the door of the room. When you are certain all of the negativity is gathered in one place, visualize it being removed from your home. In my case, the vacuum cleaner sucks up all the negativity and disposes of it. At one time, I used to visualize a giant broom sweeping all the negativity out of the door, and then out of the house. Any visualization exercise that enables you to experience the elimination of negativity will work well.

Sacred Space

Any part of the house that is used for a specific purpose will gradually develop its own energy. You can sense this in different places you visit. Your bank, for instance, will have an entirely different feel to it than your local supermarket, even though they may have many customers who use both. Similarly, a church will engender different feelings from those produced by a school.

Any part of your home that is used for a spiritual purpose will develop its own strength and energy, and this can be extremely useful in psychically protecting the home. A shrine or altar is a good way of doing this. Even displaying something small that represents your belief system will provide protection.

You need to ensure that any area you designate will be used solely for its spiritual purpose. Consequently, a table that is used as an altar should not also be used as a place to deposit groceries or items of clothing.

Your sacred space does not necessarily need to be inside the house. If you have a garden, you might establish a magic circle, or possibly construct a cairn of stones. These will gain energy from the rituals held there, and this will provide protection for everyone living in the house. The pyramid shape of a stone cairn symbolically connects the physical and spiritual worlds.

Creating a cairn of stones can be a ritual in itself. All you need are enough stones to create it. These do not need to be special stones. Any stones that appeal to you will work well.

Clear the ground on which you intend to build your cairn. Think about your need and desire for protection while holding one of the stones in your cupped hands. Consciously impart some of your personal energy into the stone, and then place it on the ground. Repeat this with the next stone, and continue thinking of your need for protection as you continue adding stones until you have built them up into a small pile. Keep adding stones until you sense that it is complete. Gently rest your dominant hand on the top stone and thank the cairn for providing you and your loved ones with protection. Visit your cairn regularly to thank it for helping you.

Many years ago, I visited a remote beach and found someone had erected four cairns just above the high water mark. They indicated the four cardinal directions. I assume someone had erected them to mark out a magic circle, and had left them there as a gift to the nature spirits.

Feng Shui

Feng shui is the ancient Chinese art of living in harmony with your environment. Protecting your home and loved ones is a vital part of this. A well-protected home is one that has formations, such as buildings, hills, trees or other vegetation, to subliminally protect the back and sides of the house. Ideally, the land in front of the house should be open and sloping slightly away from the house, but also looking towards hills or other properties. The front is unprotected if the view continues on to the horizon.

The house should not be situated in the lowest or highest part of a valley. This is because negative energy gathers at the lowest spot, and a house situated on the highest spot is exposed and unprotected.

Avoid living in a house that is dwarfed by neighboring houses, as the larger property will absorb all the good energy.

Sharp objects pointing towards your home are considered harmful as they focus negative energy in your direction. Large tree branches, especially from dead trees, are good examples, as are jagged rocks, corners of neighboring houses, TV antennas and large signs. It is especially dangerous if the sharp objects are pointing toward your front door.

Shiny objects that reflect light toward your home are also considered negative. The windows and walls of large buildings can sometimes reflect light at neighboring properties. Satellite dishes and stainless steel sculptures can do the same.

Fortunately, there is a remedy for almost every negative influence in feng shui. You can repel any negativity pointing in your direction by placing a small mirror to reflect the negativity back where it came from. Make sure that the object you are repelling can be clearly seen inside the mirror.

If the back and sides of your property are not protected you can plant a row of trees or erect a fence to provide the necessary protection. Fences and hedges can also be used to hide any objects pointing towards your home.

The front door of your home should appear welcoming. It should be well lit, uncluttered, and easy to find. The entrance should be protected from the elements. It's not much fun to get drenched with rain while looking for your keys. You also don't want your guests to get wet while waiting for you to open the door.

As we spend about a third of our lives asleep in bed, the bedroom is one of the most important rooms in feng shui. We need to feel comfortable, safe, and protected while we are asleep. Consequently, the bed needs to be placed in such a position that you can easily see anyone who comes into the room while you are lying in bed. Ideally, you don't want to turn your head more than forty-five degrees to see who is coming in. The best placement for the bed is usually diagonally across from the door.

Guardian of the Home

A guardian of the home is a small statue or ornament that acts as the spirit of your home. Choose something that you find attractive, and which exemplifies the qualities you feel necessary to guard your home. You might choose an animal, such as a dog or cat. You might prefer an angel, a warrior, or another god.

Once you have found something suitable, prepare a suitable place in your home for it. Make a small ceremony about welcoming it into your home, and tell it why you obtained it. Say that you are confident it will protect your home, and to thank it you will make regular offerings of flowers, crystals, and incense.

Initially, the statue or figurine you bought will have little protective power, but as you nurture it by talking to it and giving it small gifts, it will gain power and energy, and become a valuable guardian of your home.

Protective Plants

Plants have been used for protection purposes throughout history. The oldest surviving medical book in Old English dates back to about 950 CE. It is in three volumes, and is called the *Leech Book of Bald*, though as it is a copy of an earlier original, it is not known if the original was written by Bald, or if he simply copied it. The longest chapter in the third volume of his book was devoted to Elf-shot, or elf disease.[7] Any unexplainable illnesses or deaths in humans or animals were said to be caused by elves. Consequently, herbs and other plants were used to protect people and livestock from elf disease.

Plants that had a strong smell, such as artemisia, chives, garlic, leeks, lilies, mugwort, and onions, were hung over windows and doors. Sometimes they were also burned as incense.

Onions were especially useful, and were frequently hung in rooms to attract and absorb any negative energies and disease that would otherwise harm the occupants.

An interesting spell could also be performed with onions. If someone was experiencing a psychic attack or was surrounded by negativity, he or she could peel three small onions and hang them up in three different rooms of his or her home. The onions should be attached to the ceiling with loops of red thread that pass through the center of each onion, and left for seven nights. This gives them plenty of time to absorb all the negativity in the house. After this time, the onions should be taken down and burned outdoors in a bonfire. Alternatively, the onions can be tossed into a running stream, or any other body of moving water. This spell is extremely powerful, and will remove all the negativity. However, if the psychic attack is a particularly vicious one, this spell should be repeated to ensure success.

The elder was considered a highly protective plant, and was planted close to houses to enable them to receive its protective benefits.

The eleventh century *Herbarium of Pseudo-Apuleius* advised people to hang mugwort over the door of their home. If they did, "there may not any man damage the house."[8] The same book also recommended alyssum, betony, birthwort, horehound, peony, and yarrow as protection, especially against the evil eye.

Angelica was considered extremely useful for protecting the home and family. In 1656, William Coles wrote that you would be protected from all evil if you carried the roots of angelica with you.[9]

St. John's wort has always been considered a powerful protective plant. It is also known as hypericum, which comes from a Greek word that means, "to protect." St. John's wort was the first plant to be hung in homes on St. John's Eve (June 23rd), along with birch, fennel, white lilies, and orpine.

The root of the daffodil was also hung up in the house to ward off any evil spirits. Usually, it was wrapped in white cloth. It could also be wrapped in a clean white handkerchief and carried in a pocket.

Although much of this is folklore, many people still enjoy having protective plants in their gardens because they may be continuing a family tradition, they like the particular plants, or they gain a sense of security from having them in their gardens.

Gardens are considered special places where people can relax and commune with nature. A friend of mine calls his garden his "sanctuary." Although he spends countless hours working in his garden, he finds the labor relaxing and rewarding. It is, in effect, his escape from his busy everyday life.

Gardens also have holy and mystical connotations that possibly date all the way back to the Garden of Eden. The magical associations attributed to different plants appear in the folklore of most traditions. The charming belief that flower fairies protect gardens and all growing things, seems more than a folk tradition when you look at the large number of magnificent gardens around the world that have been created with the help of devas and fairies. Findhorn in Scotland and Perelandra in Virginia are two good examples.[10]

Charms made from herbs and other plants have always been worn or carried for a variety of purposes, including protection. Garlic is probably the best-known example, as almost everyone has heard that garlic wards off vampires. Even today, some Chinese, Greek, and Jewish grandmothers give their infant grandchildren a clove of garlic to ward off the evil eye.[11]

Vervain is related to the planet Venus. Consequently, although it was carried as an herbal charm for protection, it was also used to attract love and romance.

Herbal charms consist of a small quantity of the herb carried in a colored bag. The color of the bag is determined by the purpose of the charm. For protection purposes, the best colors are white, red, green, and violet.

Here are some of the most common trees that are planted for protection purposes:

Bay
The bay tree is believed to protect the home and garden from floods and fires.

Beech
The beech tree encourages tolerance and understanding of others. It provides the necessary strength to stand up for your beliefs. The beech tree provides good

luck and protection. Consequently, it has always been a popular wood for magic wands and lucky charms.

Birch

The birch tree is said to grow in paradise, where it is always summer. The birch is said to bring luck to anyone who lives nearby, and is one of the three most fortunate trees to have close to your home. (The other two are maple and oak.) The birch is also said to be the wife of the oak tree, and it is considered especially fortunate when both are found close together. Birch twigs are used to drive away evil spirits.

Cedar

The cedar tree is highly protective of the home and surroundings. It can also be used for emotional healing. People used to believe its wood was indestructible and the tree was immortal. Because of this, the cedar has always been considered a good source of protection.

Cypress

The cypress increases love of home and family and strengthens the family unit. It is sometimes known as "the Christian tree," as it symbolizes stoicism and standing up for what is right and true. It provides strength against any form of attack.

Elder

The elder is considered a guardian tree that protects the whole family. It is a tree of regeneration and symbolizes life energy, as it grows quickly from any part. It wards off evil spirits, and branches of elder were frequently hung at the entrances of houses and farm buildings to provide protection. However, the branches had to be found on the ground, as it was considered bad luck to chop down an elder tree.

Elm

The elm encourages nature spirits to look after the garden and home. It provides strength to the family.

Hawthorn

Hawthorn and yew trees are believed to attract beneficial fairies who will protect the home and garden. At one time, hawthorn leaves were strewn in cradles to protect the babies from witches.

Hazel

The ancient druids considered the hazel to be a tree of beauty, knowledge, wisdom, and fruitfulness. The ancient Chaldeans and Egyptians made magic wands from it. Hazel twigs should be kept above the fireplace to protect the home. Even today, many people carry a hazel twig, as they act as a charm to make all their dreams come true.

Holly

Holly is considered a lucky tree, as it provides vitality and happiness. It also protects the home from all forms of negativity. Many people carry holly berries with them for protection and to ward off any negative energies.

Oak

The oak was the holy tree of the druids. It provides peace and harmony for the household. The oak symbolizes steadfastness, strength, and courage.

Acorns are used as highly effective protective charms. One acorn provides general protection, but three acorns are supposed to be even better, as they keep you youthful in appearance and outlook.

Pine

In Japan, decorations known as *kadomatsu* (literally "gate pine") are seen around the New Year outside of businesses and people's homes. These decorations consist of bamboo stalks and pine branches and serve as temporary housing for *kami* (spirits) for the new year; they offer protection and luck. Arrangements vary, but the elements must remain the same: three bias-cut bamboo stalks representing heaven, earth, and humanity, with the "heaven" stalk being the highest. Pine branches are tucked in the bottom and can be of any length, but should not overwhelm the bamboo. The stalks are bound with fresh rope and placed in a freshly woven straw mat. *Kadomatsu* are always displayed in pairs, representing male and female.

Rowan

The rowan tree, also known as mountain ash, blesses and protects people who live in its vicinity. It is traditionally the tree of the Goddess. Legend says that fairies protect any garden that contains a rowan tree. Witches and evil spirits are said to detest the rowan tree, and go out of their way to avoid it. Rowan trees were planted close to homes to protect them from lightning and to provide good luck to the household. They were also planted in cemeteries to protect visitors from ghosts. Boats made from rowan were also popular, as the wood provided protection on the water.

Flowers and Trees of the Zodiac

Certain flowers and trees are said to protect people of different zodiac signs. The main ones are:

Aries

Flowers and herbs: bay laurel, cinnamon, clove, clover, coriander, dragon's blood, feverfew, garlic, ginger, gorse, honeysuckle, juniper, nasturtium, peppermint, sweet pea, thistle, wild rose

Trees: chestnut, holly, thorn

Taurus

Flowers and herbs: cinquefoil, coltsfoot, columbine, daisy, forget-me-nots, foxglove, lily of the valley, lime, lovage, mandrake, myrtle blossom, onion, poppy, primula, rose, sage, sorrel, violet, wintergreen

Trees: almond, apple, ash, cherry, fig, myrtle, pear, sycamore, walnut

Gemini

Flowers and herbs: angelica, bergamot, betony, dill, fern, honeysuckle, iris, lavender, leek, lily of the valley, mint, myrtle, oregano, snapdragon, thyme, vervain

Trees: chestnut, elder, filbert, hazel

Cancer

Flowers and herbs: anise, lemon balm, caraway, catnip, chervil, convolvulus, dill, geranium, honesty, hyssop, jasmine, larkspur, olive, peppermint, poppy, privet, watercress, waterlily, white rose

Trees: maple, sycamore, willow

Leo

Flowers and herbs: almond, arnica, camomile, camphor, cowslip, cyclamen, daffodil, forsythia, heliotrope, lavender, lemon, marigold, mistletoe, passionflower, peony, sunflower

Trees: bay, citrus trees, laurel, oak, olive, palm, pine

Virgo
Flowers and herbs: barley, bean, buttercup, chicory, cornflower, ginseng, houndstongue, Madonna lily, pansy, parsnip, patchouli, rosemary, sandalwood

Trees: elder, hazel, and all nut-bearing trees

Libra
Flowers and herbs: agrimony, aloe, apple blossom, bluebell, carnation, cucumber, dandelion, foxglove, hellebore, hydrangea, love-in-a-mist, parsley, rose, strawberry, violet

Trees: almond, apple, ash, myrtle, plum, poplar, walnut

Scorpio
Flowers and herbs: acacia, amaranth, basil, lesser celandine, chrysanthemum, cowslip, geranium, ivy, milfoil, musk, pennyroyal, purple heather, rhododendrum, valerian

Trees: blackthorn, holly, whitethorn

Sagittarius
Flowers and herbs: carnation, cedarwood, dandelion, elder, eucalyptus, geranium, hawthorn, narcissus, nutmeg, sage, thistle, wallflower

Trees: ash, beech, birch, chestnut, mulberry, oak, poplar, rowan

Capricorn

Flowers and herbs: amaranthus, belladonna, benzoin, buttercup, carnation, cassia, comfrey, flaxseed, ivy, marjoram, nightshade, pansy, plantain, rue, snowdrop, Solomon's seal, witch hazel

Trees: cypress, elm, holly, pine, poplar, spruce, willow, yew

Aquarius

Flowers and herbs: borage, cypress, fennel, foxglove, frankincense, gentian violet, henbane, iris, moonwort, mullein, orchid, snowdrop, St. John's wort

Tree: all fruit trees, pine

Pisces

Flowers and herbs: carnation, civet, ergot, geranium, heliotrope, daffodil, lily of the valley, lotus, poppy, verbena, violet, water lily

Tree: fig, willow

Rose Water

Rose water is a useful way to protect your home. You can buy it at many drugstores. However, it is easy to make, and I usually prefer to prepare it myself. Here is the recipe I usually use:

Place a teaspoon of rose petals into a cup of boiling water. Allow it to steep for about fifteen minutes.

Add a quarter of a cup of vodka, and stir for thirty seconds. Allow it to cool before use.

You can use rose water to trace the frames of the windows and doors in your home. I prefer to work around the house in a clockwise direction, and also trace the frames in the same direction. An acquaintance of mine keeps her rose water in a spray bottle, as this means she can spray any area she wishes quickly and easily.

Tree Hugging

When my children were growing up, I sometimes teased them when we were out in public by commenting on different trees. Each time I remarked on how attractive a tree was, they'd run, because they thought I'd embarrass them by hugging it.

Tree hugging is a form of meditation. It is also a wonderful way to release stress and to gain energy. There is no right or wrong way to hug a tree. Even touching the bark of a tree with the palm of one hand is beneficial. The most effective way I've found to hug a tree is to have my brow and heart chakras in contact with the trunk of the tree.

Choose a tree that is aesthetically pleasing to you. I usually prefer older trees, as I happen to like the energy produced by more mature trees. However, you may well prefer younger trees.

Face the tree with your legs apart. Smile at the tree for a few seconds, and then lean into the tree to allow your chest, home of the heart chakra, to contact the trunk of the tree. Place your arms around the tree and hug it gently. Rest your forehead against the trunk, to allow your brow chakra to contact the tree. Take a slow, deep breath and close your eyes.

Breathe slowly and deeply, using your diaphragm, and focus on the area of your heart chakra. You will gradually experience feelings of peace and tranquility. After about thirty seconds, focus on your brow chakra for the same length of time. Alternate your attention between the two chakras for as long as you wish. Feel the energy of the tree in every part of your body that is in contact with the tree.

Continue hugging the tree for as long as you wish. When you feel ready to let go, silently thank the tree. Stroke or pat the tree goodbye. I usually wave goodbye to it as well.

Some people energize all their chakras by standing with their backs against the trunk of the tree and hugging the tree behind their backs. I also do this at times, but usually I prefer to face the tree as I hug it. Another way of gaining energy from the tree is to sit with your back against the tree.

All of these methods provide you with strength and energy, allowing you to face any situation in a calm state of mind.

Rory's Experience

I have known Rory for most of my life. He is charming, gregarious, and enthusiastic. He's also a highly successful businessman. He has a delightful wife and three adult children who are all doing well. He has never shown any interest in psychic matters, though he's always been encouraging and supportive about my efforts to make a living as a writer of books on these subjects.

Rory and his wife, Judy, move house every five or six years. Their friends all love the wonderful housewarming parties they hold to celebrate each move. Rory and Judy enjoy entertaining and also hold smaller parties to celebrate the change of the seasons.

A year or so ago, I was having lunch with Rory and happened to mention one of his housewarming parties and how much fun they were.

"You know why we have them," Rory said. He laughed at the expression on my face. "Yes, we have them to bless the house and to encourage the spirits of the house to look after us."

"Why haven't you mentioned this before?" I asked.

Rory laughed again. "Well, it's not the sort of thing you discuss with everyone, and I sort of assumed you'd know anyway."

I shook my head. "It never occurred to me. We've never discussed anything along these lines before."

"Well, now you know."

"And the parties you have at all the solstices?"

"They reaffirm our attachment to the house. Judy believes they help protect the house."

"And you?"

Rory shrugged. "I always love a party. And, yes, I think any fun and laughter inside the home helps protect it and make it strong. People always say our homes have good vibes, and I'm sure the parties help create that."

In the next chapter, we'll look at how meditation can be used to provide protection. This is a completely different way of providing psychic protection for yourself and others.

Meditative Protection

People have practiced meditation for thousands of years. A four-thousand-year-old seal discovered in the remains of an ancient city called Mohenjodaro (in present-day Pakistan) shows a figure seated in a cross-legged meditation posture. This is the earliest evidence of the practice of meditation.[1]

The ultimate goal of meditation is to become one with the Divine. However, most people meditate to experience feelings of peace and calm in mind, body, and spirit. Meditation has many benefits, including greater self-esteem, better health, enhanced creativity, closer relationships, and self-knowledge. It also enables people to develop their spiritual and psychic (especially clairvoyant and precognitive) skills.

In the 1970s, researchers discovered the impressive health benefits that meditation provides. Professor Herbert Benson of the Harvard Medical School found that meditation reduces blood pressure, heart rate, breathing rate, and muscle tension. As a result, this slowed down metabolism. Later studies revealed that meditation also helps people suffering from anxiety, depression, stress, headaches, insomnia, and chronic pain.

Meditation plays an important role in many religions, including Buddhism, Hinduism, Sufism, and Taoism. It also features in the Jewish and Christian mystical traditions.

Meditation also enables you to take control of your thoughts, replacing long-standing negative thought patterns with positive thoughts of strength, confidence, and protection.

To experiment with meditation, all you need do is find a quiet, warm space where you won't be interrupted for at least thirty minutes. Traditionally, meditation was done by sitting on the ground in the lotus position. However, you can meditate in any position that is comfortable for you. You might like to sit in a straight-backed chair, with your feet on the ground and your hands resting on your thighs. Alternatively, you might like to rest your hands palms up, one on top of the other, in your lap. You may prefer to lie on your back with your hands by your sides. If you prefer this position, experiment with lying on the floor, rather than on a bed. I find that if I meditate on a bed, I'm likely to fall asleep during the meditation. This doesn't happen when I lie down on the floor or outdoors on the ground.

Wear loose-fitting clothes. Use a pillow and a blanket, if necessary. It's important to be both comfortable and warm. You might like to play meditation music. If you do, choose something quiet and gentle, with no discernible melody. I occasionally play meditation music but usually prefer to meditate in silence.

Become aware of your breathing, and take several slow, deep breaths. Once you feel yourself becoming relaxed, focus on different parts of your body, and allow them to relax, until your entire body is completely relaxed.

Once you reach this state, you'll be able to make positive suggestions to yourself that you are strong and in control of your own life. You'll be able to affirm that your mind, body, and spirit are all protected by divine love.

When you are ready to return to your normal, everyday life, all you need do is slowly count from one to five. Open your eyes, stretch, and relax for a minute or two before getting up and continuing with your day.

The more you practice this exercise, the easier it will become. It is frustratingly easy to become distracted by outside sounds, or even random thoughts that pop into your mind. Whenever you find yourself becoming distracted, gently refocus on your goal, and allow yourself to relax and concentrate again.

To help make the process easier, you might like to record this script and allow it to guide you through the process. When you first start experimenting with meditation, it is much easier to follow a guided meditation than it is to do it entirely yourself.

Take a nice, slow, deep breath and close your eyes as you exhale. Allow the muscles around your eyes to relax. In fact, just let all those muscles relax. Each breath you take makes you more and more relaxed. Enjoy the feeling of pleasant relaxation as you drift deeper and deeper with each easy breath. Take a slow, deep breath now, hold it for a moment, and let it out slowly. You enjoy taking slow, deep breaths as they help you drift deeper and deeper into total relaxation.

Focus on your left foot now, and let the muscles in your toes relax. Once you feel your toes are completely relaxed, allow the pleasant relaxation to drift through your left foot and up to the ankle. There's no hurry. Take your time, and allow the pleasant feelings of relaxation to spread into every cell of your left foot and up to your ankle.

Allow that pleasant relaxation to drift up your leg, relaxing your calf muscles, your knee and your thigh, until you feel your entire left leg is totally relaxed.

Now, focus on your right foot, and allow the muscles in your toes to relax. Feel that pleasant relaxation as it drifts through your right foot and up to your ankle. Once your foot feels loose and limp and totally relaxed, allow the relaxation to gently drift up your right leg, until both legs are totally, completely relaxed.

Allow the pleasant relaxation to drift into your abdomen, up to your chest, and into your shoulders. Feel the relaxation drifting down your left arm, all the way to the tips of your fingers. Totally, completely, absolutely relaxed. It's a wonderful feeling. Allow the relaxation to drift down your right arm, all the way to the tips of your fingers.

When your whole body feels totally relaxed, allow the relaxation to drift through your neck and into your face. Allow the fine muscles around your eyes to relax, and then feel the pleasant relaxation drifting up to the top of your head.

You feel totally relaxed throughout your entire body.

Allow another wave of pleasant relaxation to drift through your body, starting with your feet, and gradually moving right through your body to the top of your head. As you breathe slowly and deeply, and as you relax, you enjoy the feeling of total tranquility and relaxation in every cell of your body. Every part of your body is loose, limp and so, so relaxed. It's a wonderful feeling to be drifting into this state of total relaxation where nothing can disturb or bother you.

Although you feel totally relaxed now, you know you can go even deeper into this wonderful, pleasant world of total relaxation. To help you do this, imagine that you're standing on the crest of a small hill gazing out at the most magnificent view you've ever seen. In your mind, look around and spend a moment or two enjoying the peace, quiet, and utter tranquility of the scene. Feel the warmth of the sun, and notice the slight trace of a breeze on your face. A few birds fly high above you, and you can hear the rhythmic beating of their wings. Look down, and you'll see ten wooden steps leading down to a small level area where you can lie on the soft grass and relax even more.

Place your hand on the handrail, and double your relaxation with each step you take as you slowly go down the wooden steps.

Ten. Double your relaxation as you take the first step.

Nine. Take another step. Drifting down, deeper and deeper into total peace and relaxation.

Eight. Drifting down, feeling wonderful and so, so relaxed.

Seven. Doubling your relaxation yet again as you step down. You're allowing yourself to feel more limp, loose and relaxed than you've ever been before.

Six. Another step. Lower and lower, deeper and deeper into pleasant relaxation.

Five. You're halfway down now.

Four. Enjoying the feel of the wooden steps beneath your feet as you double your relaxation once more.

Three . . . two . . . and one. As you step off onto the beautiful, warm grass, you feel so incredibly relaxed and at peace. You can smell the sweet grass as you sit down, and you feel its gentle texture with your hands. It's so comfortable that you lie down on the soft grass, and any remaining stress and strain flows right out of you and into the ground, while you remain calm, relaxed, and serene on the nice, warm grass.

And in this nice, calm, peaceful, relaxed state, you can look at every aspect of your life in a calm and detached manner. You realize that you are in total control of your life, and you can do anything you set your mind to. Whether you are aware of it or not, you are protected at all times by divine light. This divine light keeps you safe and protected from harm. All positive thoughts and emotions are attracted to you, and at the same time all negativity is repelled.

Whenever you feel the need for additional protection, all you need do is close your eyes, take three slow, deep breaths, and visualize yourself in your special, secret place where everything is absolutely perfect. In your imagination now, see yourself walking down a beautiful staircase and into the most magnificent room you have ever seen. It seems light and spacious. The walls contain a selection of beautiful paintings, and the furniture looks comfortable and inviting. The temperature of the room is perfect. Feel the texture of the carpet beneath your feet as you walk across the room. Take deep breaths of the beautiful, fresh air. Sit down on one of the comfortable chairs and allow yourself to sink into it. You've never felt so relaxed, or comfortable, or safe. In this pleasant, tranquil state, you accept and recognize yourself as the wonderful person you are.

Look upwards and notice a pure white light descending onto and around you, filling you with energy and feelings of security and happiness. As you watch, the entire room fills with this pure, protective light. With each breath you take, you fill your body with divine, healing, protective light. This white light protects you internally and externally from all forms of negativity. It surrounds you with security and love. It's an impenetrable wall that protects you and keeps you safe at all times. You feel a sense of happiness and well-being in every cell of your body, as you know that you are totally protected every day and every night. Everywhere you go from now on, you'll feel a sense of additional security, knowing that you are totally protected from any form of psychic attack.

Whenever you feel the need for additional protection, all you need do is close your eyes, take three slow, deep breaths, and visualize yourself in your secret room where everything is perfect and you feel totally protected and safe. Spend a few seconds in this special room and, when you open your eyes, you'll feel secure and in total control of the situation, no matter what it may be. Situations that you used to find stressful or difficult in the past will now seem effortless, as you'll remain calm and relaxed, secure in the knowledge that you're constantly surrounded by *a divine light that gives you confidence as well as protection. You're transformed now. You've created a whole new positive reality for yourself. You are confident, independent, determined, and secure. You're in control and able to handle any situation in a calm and relaxed manner.*

You can visit your special secret room whenever you wish. After each visit you'll feel invigorated, empowered, and able to handle anything that life might send in your direction. You feel strong, grounded, safe, secure, and protected at all times. You feel strong, grounded, safe, secure, and protected at all times. The white light of protection is always with you.

And now, totally protected and revitalized in mind, body and spirit, it's time to return to the present. You'll gradually return to full conscious awareness on the count of five. One, gaining energy and feeling wonderful. Two, feeling full of confidence and energy. Three, recalling everything that transpired during this meditation. Four, feeling absolutely wonderful, and five, eyes opening and feeling great.

Some people like to record a script and play it in bed at night, as it helps them relax and fall asleep. If you choose to do this, you can change the counting at the end to enable you to enjoy a good night's sleep. You might say:

And now, totally protected and revitalized in mind, body and spirit, it's time to return to the present. You'll gradually return to full conscious awareness on the count of five. If you are listening to this in bed at night, on the count of five you'll roll over and enjoy a pleasant, peaceful and restful night's sleep. Any other time you are listening to these words, you'll open your eyes on the count of five feeling totally revitalized and in full control. And now the counting begins. One, gaining energy and feeling wonderful. Two, feeling full of confidence and energy. Three, recalling everything that transpired during this meditation. Four, feeling absolutely wonderful, and five, eyes opening and feeling great.

Remember to ground yourself after meditating. Go outside and touch the earth. Eat or drink something, and do something physical to bring you back to reality.

If you are experiencing stress or a prolonged psychic attack, you might like to add a bubble of protection to your meditation:

You are calm and relaxed at all times, as you are totally surrounded by a clear bubble of protection that keeps you safe from harm and stress and pressure. Any pressure or stress or negativity of any sort will be deflected away from you by your bubble of protection. It simply bounces off and away from you, while you remain calm and free from stress inside. Your bubble protects you from any and all pressure and negativity. Visualize yourself now in a scene that might have been difficult for you in the past. See yourself handling it easily now that you're surrounded by your bubble of protection. You can actually watch the negativity bounce off and away from you. Off and away. You are totally protected, safe and secure inside your bubble of protection. You are now immune to any form of antagonism, stress, jealousy, envy, or psychic attack, as you are completely surrounded and safe inside your invisible bubble of protection. You can face any situation at all in a calm and relaxed manner, because you are totally protected, and completely free from stress.

You might also like to include your home, family, and other special people in your life in your meditation. You might say:

You're safe, secure, and protected inside your clear bubble of protection, and now you're going to extend your bubble of protection. With each easy breath you take your bubble of protection expands more and more until it includes your home and everyone you love and cherish. You can see (name the people you want to protect)

safely inside this huge bubble, enjoying all the
protection and security they need.

And if any of them need to move outside
your bubble of protection for any reason, they'll
be surrounded in a bubble of their own. In your
mind's eye you can see them leaving your bubble
of protection, and you can watch them safely
cocooned in their own bubble as they head off
to do whatever it is they need to do. And when
they return, they'll easily merge into your bubble
again.

Your home, your family, and loved ones, are
all safe, secure, and fully protected. Your home,
family and loved ones are totally protected.

Meditating with Crystals

Crystals are frequently used to enhance meditation,
and can even be used to induce it. You can use whatever crystals you wish. However, the ones that are
most frequently used are amethyst, and clear, smoky
or rose quartz.

Prepare for your meditation in your usual way,
and either hold the crystal or place it where you can
see it. Gaze at the crystal and take several slow, deep
breaths. Pay attention to the shape, color, and beauty
of your crystal. Allow your eyes to close as soon as
they feel heavy, and focus on your breathing. Feel
yourself gradually sinking into a relaxed, meditative

state. Allow your aura to expand to encompass the crystal, and feel the crystalline energy in every part of your body. Hold this feeling for as long as you can. You might even feel yourself becoming as one with the crystal. You might ask it questions, or simply enjoy being part of it.

When you feel ready, become aware of your breathing again, take three slow, deep breaths and open your eyes. Thank the crystal for the insights it gave you. Remain sitting or lying down for a minute or two, and then get up. Perform some form of grounding, before carrying on with your day.

If you have a collection of crystals, you can arrange them into a pattern or mandala and meditate while gazing at them. Alternatively, you could surround yourself with a circle of crystals and meditate inside them.

Now that you have learned how to relax quickly and easily, you are ready to move on to methods of handling deliberate psychic attack.

twelve

How to Ward Off a Psychic Attack

A psychic attack is a deliberate paranormal assault that a person or group commits on someone else. Its intention is to cause stress, worry, illness, and even sometimes, death. When aborigines "point the bone" at someone, they are, in effect, psychically attacking the person. There have been many recorded instances of victims wasting away and dying as a result of attacks of this sort. Pushing pins and nails into a wax doll that symbolizes the victim is another form of deliberate psychic attack, as the intention is to cause harm to the victim.

In 1455, nuns from a convent at Wennigsen, near Hanover, psychically attacked a group of officials who had visited their convent with the intention of reforming them. After a great deal of argument and discussion, which failed to resolve the problem, the nuns attempted to psychically attack the officials.

They lay down with their arms spread out to form the shape of a cross and began chanting the anthem commonly used in burial services, *In the midst of life we are in death.* The intention of chanting these words was serious: the nuns wanted to kill the unwanted officials.[1]

Probably the most famous example of a deliberate psychic attack is the curse made by Jacques de Molay (1243–1314), the last grand master of the Knights Templars. On March 18, 1314, as he was about to be burned at the stake outside the Cathedral of Notre Dame in Paris, Jacques de Molay swore an oath of revenge on his persecutors, Pope Clement V and King Philip IV of France, telling them they would join him within a year. The pope died from dysentery on April 20, 1314, and King Philip died on November 29, 1314, both well within the year.[2]

In the early eighteenth century, M'Alister Indre, a Scottish chief, was cursed. After a fight with a neighboring clan, M'Alister hanged the two sons of a widow outside her home. M'Alister laughed at the broken-hearted mother, but that evening she cursed him, saying, "I suffer now, but you shall suffer always. You have made me childless, but you and yours shall be heirless for ever. Never shall there be a son to the house of M'Alister."

This curse was fulfilled, as not long afterwards, M'Alister was captured by the English and put to death, leaving his wife childless.[3]

Psychic attacks can come from anywhere, at any time. You can become a victim of this even if you consciously try to get on with everyone in your life. Strangers might curse you if they see you as being different from them. Others might envy your perceived success. Jealousy and resentment are common reasons for psychic attack. If you are promoted at work, someone who had hoped to receive the promotion instead of you might psychically attack you. Anyone who is in competition with you for any reason whatsoever could potentially decide to psychically attack you. Politics rears its head even in small groups and clubs. Power struggles are a common reason for psychic attacks.

Although it's a popular subject in fiction, a deliberate, intentional, prolonged psychic attack is extremely rare. I suppose it is possible for two magicians to psychically attack each other, but as it would take an enormous amount of time and effort, not to mention negative energy, I doubt that any serious magician would consider it worthwhile. After all, if the person being attacked had protected him or her self, any negative energy would simply be deflected away, and the attacking magician would have to cope with a threefold return of huge amounts of negative energy. This means the person performing the psychic attack would be affected much more than the person being attacked.

However, minor and subconscious psychic attacks are common. There are a number of things you can do if you discover you are suffering a psychic attack:

1. Ground yourself. Go outdoors and touch the earth. Spend time in a park or garden to strengthen every cell of your body.

2. Strengthen your aura with meditations, visualizations and exercise.

3. Send love to everyone you know, both friend and foe.

4. Take salt baths. Some people like to include two parts baking soda to one part salt when they experience a psychic attack.

5. Bolster your self-esteem by constantly telling yourself what a wonderful, caring, and considerate person you are.

6. Surround yourself with white light and a bubble of protection.

7. Do something physical. This serves three purposes. It recharges your aura, relieves stress, and the endorphins produced provide additional protection.

8. Pay close attention to your intuition.

9. If it is a part of your belief system, call on a higher power and ask for help. You might call on the universal life source, your guardian angel or your spirit guide. Praying, and asking other people to pray for you, is a highly effective method of defense.

10. Avoid all contact with the person or people you suspect.

11. Eat healthy food to keep your strength up. A full stomach also closes down your psychic centers, providing an effective form of protection.

12. Avoid sugary foods and drinks. Soda drinks are not good for you at the best of times, but are especially bad when you're experiencing a psychic attack. These foods and drinks raise your blood sugar levels, creating a roller coaster effect of ups (the blood sugar rush) and downs. Sugary foods can seem seductive, as they make you feel good temporarily, but you must avoid them, as they make you an easy target for whoever is psychically attacking you.

13. Drink plenty of water. Bless the water before drinking it.

14. Laugh as much as possible. If necessary, rent comedy movies and DVDs of stand-up comics. Laughter releases endorphins and promotes feelings of well-being.

15. Spend as much time as possible with people you love. Avoid being alone for long periods of time.

16. Buy new clothes. It is advisable to do so because your old clothes are full of your energy. If it's not practical to replace your clothes, wash or dry-clean them. You should also repair anything that is damaged or missing. Replacing a missing button, fixing a broken zipper, and repairing a torn seam will all help protect you.

17. Nurture yourself in some way. Enjoy a massage, visit an art museum, play a sport, or do something you haven't done before, purely for the fun of it.

18. Most psychic attacks occur during the night. Consequently, it is a good idea to sleep in a different bedroom than usual during a prolonged attack.

Verbal Attacks

Many years ago, when I was making my living as a hypnotherapist, a lady left a message on my answering machine saying she wanted to make an appointment. When I called back, a man answered the phone. Because many people visit hypnotherapists for private problems, I was unable to tell other people who answered my return phone calls what I was calling about. Consequently, in this case, I gave the man my name, and asked to speak to the lady. As soon as I did this, he started abusing me. He seemed to think I was trying to forge an intimate relationship with his girlfriend. In highly colorful language, he told me not to contact his girlfriend again, and hung up. I was stunned for a while, but then saw the humorous side of the situation. I telepathically sent peace and love to him, as he desperately needed it. He was obviously extremely insecure, jealous, and suspicious. Over the years, I've sometimes wondered how long that relationship lasted. This experience shows that verbal attacks can occur any time, often without any provocation whatsoever.

A verbal attack is a form of psychic attack as negativity is being aimed directly at you. Verbal attacks frequently come from left field, when you least expect them. They can be devastating, especially if delivered by someone you considered a friend.

Verbal attacks occur in many forms. Someone may threaten or intimidate you. An insensitive boss might rebuke you in front of fellow workers. You might learn that people are gossiping about you behind your back. Most victims of verbal abuse stifle their emotions and suffer in silence. Fortunately, that is not necessary.

There are a number of things you can do to handle verbal abuse.

1. Take slow, deep breaths. This sends oxygen to the brain, and helps relieve the sudden tension the abuse creates throughout your body.

2. Strengthen your aura, using the techniques described in chapter 6.

3. Do something physical as soon as possible after the attack. A punching bag would be perfect, but a brisk walk is almost as good.

4. Vent, rage, cry, and scream in the privacy of your own home. You don't want to give the person who has verbally abused you the satisfaction of seeing how hurt you are, but you should certainly let off steam as soon as possible.

5. Make sure you get enough sleep. It can be hard to sleep when you're experiencing an attack. Practice the meditation exercises in

chapter 11 in bed, and allow them to send you off to sleep.

6. Cleanse your home. This is useful in two ways. It involves physical activity, and while you are doing it, you can visualize all of the negativity around you fading away until it has completely vanished.

7. Once you have cleansed your home, sprinkle a few grains of salt in the corners of every room. If you live in an apartment building, sprinkle a few grains of salt at the entrance of your apartment, as well as the main entrance of the building. If you live in a house, sprinkle salt around the building, also.

8. When you are ready, and this might take a while, forgive the person who abused you. The act of forgiveness returns your personal power, and the person who abused you will no longer have any effect upon you.

Nowadays, a different form of abuse has become more prevalent. Some people hide under assumed names on Internet forums and attack others. These people are cowards who would never be brave enough to tell you in person what they're happy to publish under a pseudonym. I feel sorry for people who feel they need to act in this way. However, what they write can be hurtful, and the best remedy is to follow the suggestions for handling verbal abuse. Don't bother trying to defend yourself, as that encourages these sad people to write more. It is much more effective to keep your protection up and enjoy the company of friends and loved ones.

How to Know if You Are Being Psychically Attacked

Sometimes it will be obvious that someone is deliberately attacking you. Tom, an acquaintance of mine, received a drawing of a pentacle in the mail. His name was written around the drawing, and the sheet of paper had been roughly torn into quarters. Tom knew right away who had sent it to him. He had advertised a class on mediumship in a local paper, and someone who was already teaching similar courses took offence. The attack was vicious and prolonged, and hurt both people involved, as well as their families, and the students from both teachers. The outcome wasn't satisfactory, either. The newspaper banned both of them from advertising their courses, and Tom eventually moved to a different city. Years later, Tom told me that if he hadn't been protected, he would have suffered a nervous breakdown. I have no idea what happened to the person who instigated the attack. He stopped offering courses, and I haven't heard his name mentioned in years.

Tom knew he was under attack, as the message he received through the mail warned him.

Dion Fortune (1890–1947), the celebrated occultist and author of many books, including *Psychic Self-Defense*, wrote about her experiences after a particularly savage psychic attack. It began with feelings of unease, and "gradually progressed into a definite sense of menace and antagonism."[4] At this stage she knew someone was psychically attacking her, but had no idea who it was until she received a letter from someone she considered a friend. This "friend" had taken offence to an article Dion Fortune had published in *Occult Review* and promised further attacks if the articles continued. Dion Fortune did not mention the name of this "friend" in her book, but clearly identified her as Mrs. Moina Mathers, widow of S. L. MacGregor Mathers, one of the founders of the Hermetic Order of the Golden Dawn, in an article published in *Occult Review* in January 1933.[5]

Both Tom and Dion Fortune received letters telling them they were under attack. Most of the time, it is not likely to be as obvious as this. Fortunately, there are ways of determining whether or not you are being attacked.

The most common indication of a psychic attack is called the "hag syndrome." The victim of the attack wakes up with a crushing weight on his or her chest. The victim is also temporarily unable to move any part of his or her body. Sometimes the victim sees phantom-like shapes, smells unpleasant odors, and hears strange sounds.

The "hag syndrome" has been documented throughout history. As far back as the second century CE, Galen, the Roman physician, said it was caused by indigestion. A few hundred years ago, it was blamed on witchcraft. Sexual repression and sleeping problems have also been suggested as possible causes, but there is still no categorical explanation for the phenomenon.

Other common indications of a psychic attack are nervous exhaustion, caused by feelings of dread, hopelessness and fear, and a sudden, unexplained loss of weight. Loss of appetite, nausea, nightmares, poltergeist phenomena, and unexplained bruises and wounds on the body are also said to indicate psychic attack.

In most of these instances, the victim gradually becomes aware that he or she is being attacked. If you suspect you are a victim, you can use a pendulum to gain further information.

How to Use a Pendulum

A pendulum is simply a small weight attached to chain, cord, or thread. An impromptu pendulum can be made by suspending a ring or a paperclip on a piece of thread. Commercially made pendulums are readily available at New Age stores. You can buy pendulums in a wide variety of shapes and sizes. They can be made from almost any material, including wood, metal, crystal, and plastic. Choose a shape that is symmetrical, as this creates good balance, which makes the pendulum more sensitive and easier to use.

Once you have a pendulum, you will need to practice with it. It is best to do this on your own, unless you are experimenting with like-minded people. If you are sitting down, rest your elbow on a table and hold the pendulum between your thumb and first finger. Your elbow should be the only part of your body in contact with the table. Make sure your stomach or other hand is not touching the table. The palm of your hand should be facing downwards, and the pendulum should be hanging approximately twelve inches in front of you. If you are standing to use your pendulum, the best position is to have an angle of ninety degrees at the elbow, so that your forearm is parallel to the ground.

Swing the pendulum gently to become familiar with the movements it makes. Let it swing in different directions, as well as in circles.

Experiment by holding the pendulum in different hands. Most people prefer to hold the pendulum using their dominant hand, but some people get better results using the other hand. Experiment also by holding the thread at different lengths to determine if the pendulum moves more readily with a longer or shorter thread. Most people find between four and five inches is the best length, but again, everyone is different and you may find a shorter or longer length is better for you.

Once you become used to the feel of the pendulum, stop the movements of the weight with your free hand. When the pendulum is still, ask it which movement indicates a positive, or yes response. If you have never used a pendulum before, it might take a while to respond, and the movement is likely to be slight. Be patient. Keep thinking yes, and it will ultimately start to move. I have yet to meet anyone who cannot use a pendulum, so do not become concerned if it fails to move right away. Practice for five minutes, then put the pendulum away for a while and try again later.

The pendulum can move in a variety of directions: from side to side, backwards and forwards, and in a circular movement, both clockwise and anticlockwise. Once the pendulum has told you which movement indicates yes, ask it to indicate no, or a negative response. Follow this by asking for "I don't know" and "I don't want to answer."

Write down the movement for each response. These responses will probably remain the same for you for the rest of your life. However, you should check the responses every now and again. Quite a few people find that the responses can change, especially if they haven't used a pendulum for a while.

Now that you have become familiar with your pendulum, you can ask it anything you wish that can be answered by the four possible responses. Start by asking it questions to which you already know the answers. You might ask, "Am I female?" If you are, the pendulum should answer yes. Naturally, the answer will be no if you are male. Continue asking questions to get used to the pendulum. With practice, you'll find your pendulum responds immediately to whatever question is asked. You will also find that it makes no difference if you ask your questions silently or out loud.

Once the pendulum has demonstrated its accuracy in answering questions that you know the answers for, it is time to ask it questions that you would like to know the answers to. The pendulum is able to do this because it obtains the answers from your subconscious mind, and brings them back to your conscious mind.

It is important to remember that your pendulum is a valuable tool, and it should not be used flippantly. Ask it serious questions, and you will receive honest and correct answers. There is an exception to this, though. If you have a strong emotional involvement in the answer, the pendulum is likely to give you the response you desire. This is because your desire will always override the natural response of the pendulum.

If a pregnant woman asks a pendulum if her unborn baby will be, say, a boy, and honestly has no preference, the pendulum will answer correctly. However, if she is secretly wishing for a boy, the pendulum will confirm that, even if the unborn baby is a girl. The pendulum will respond to her desire, rather than give the correct answer.

You need to bear this in mind if you are asking your pendulum questions about a possible psychic attack. You are likely to be stressed, suspicious, and anxious. You may think you know who is attacking you, and your pendulum will confirm that, because it will be responding to your suspicions.

Consequently, you will need to find someone who is not emotionally involved to ask the pendulum questions for you. This person needs to be someone you trust implicitly. Naturally, he or she must be able to use a pendulum, but ideally should know little or nothing about the topic of psychic attack.

Write down the questions you want the person to ask, and leave the building. Go for a walk or do something else to distract you while the person asks the questions for you. Accept the answers the pendulum provides, even if they are not the answers you want or expect.

Many years ago, I knew a young lady who was convinced she was undergoing a psychic attack. She was furious when the pendulum said she wasn't, and lost a good friend by accusing someone of psychically attacking her. Her friend was innocent, which is what the pendulum had said. This young lady was overworked and highly stressed in a job she hated. She thought her feelings and emotional state were caused by a psychic attack, when in fact they were created by her work. You must accept the answers the pendulum supplies, and not constantly ask the same questions again and again in the hope of receiving a different response.

Releasing Baggage Exercise

This is a useful exercise that enables you to eliminate unwanted baggage from your life. We all tend to carry around a huge amount of unwanted stress, feelings, memories, and other baggage around with us, and these limit our lives in many ways. This exercise is also useful for eliminating unwanted people from your life. If you know the identity of the person who is psychically attacking you, you can use this exercise to remove him or her from your life. This makes him or her powerless. There is one exception. You cannot eliminate family members with a baggage release exercise. This is because they have a karmic influence on you, and the lessons they help you learn are a necessary part of your growth and development.

You should perform the baggage release regularly, as everyone picks up baggage unconsciously as they go through life. I frequently perform this exercise in bed at night.

1. Take three slow, deep breaths and allow your body to relax. I usually use the script in chapter 11 to get to the desired level of relaxation.

2. Once you are fully relaxed, move your consciousness away from your body, so you can "see" yourself lying peacefully in bed. If you find it difficult to do this, simply imagine yourself lying in bed.

3. Imagine that your physical body is morphing into a huge ball of wool. You can see different strands of wool running off in different directions. Each strand is connected to baggage you are carrying.

4. Visualize a huge pair of scissors, and see yourself cutting off all the loose strands of wool until the ball is round and smooth. You might be able to identify the strand that connects you with the person who has been psychically attacking you. If so, you'll gain enormous pleasure from cutting it, and

setting yourself free. It doesn't matter if you can't identify the specific strand. By cutting off all the baggage, you'll automatically free yourself from whoever it is.

5. Check to make sure that every loose strand has been cut off. Allow yourself to morph back to your normal self again.

6. If you are doing this in bed at night, allow yourself to drift off to sleep. You'll enjoy a particularly good night's sleep, as you'll be free from all the problems you've let go. There's no need to concern yourself with them any more. If you are doing this exercise during the day, become aware of your surroundings, take three, slow deep breaths, and open your eyes. Lie still for about sixty seconds, and then get up and continue with your day.

Remember that a deliberate psychic attack is rare. If you make an effort to live a good life and get along well with others, you are most unlikely to ever be attacked in this way.

Now it's time to learn how to use the powers of magic to gain complete, overall psychic protection.

thirteen

Protection Magic

According to the occultist and author Aleister Crowley (1875–1947), magic is "the science or art of causing change to occur in conformity with Will." In other words, magic is the art of manipulating energy. You have done this many times, even though you may not have called it magic. Whenever you set a goal for yourself, and then follow through and achieve it, you are "causing change to occur in conformity with will." This means you have the ability to create what you want using the power of your mind. Consequently, whatever you demand from the universe, the universe will provide. This is an example of the law of cause and effect.

There is nothing supernatural about this. Everyone on this planet possesses enormous reserves of personal power. The only problem is that most people fail to recognize this. The people who succeed are the ones who consciously use this personal power.

Magic is extremely powerful and can be used for both good and ill. If you intend to use magic, you need to be absolutely certain that your intention will not adversely harm anyone, as whatever you send out into the universe will come back threefold. If you send out good wishes to the universe, three times that amount will come back to you. Of course, if you send out bad wishes, three times that amount will also come back to you.

Wiccans call protective magic *warding*. This is derived from the expression "to ward off evil." They perform magic to ward off the evil eye and illnesses, and to protect themselves, loved ones, and their homes. Of course, not only Wiccans use warding for protection. A common example of warding, or protection magic, is the Roman Catholic practice of making the sign of the cross. The feng shui practice of using mirrors to repel potential evil is another example of protection magic.

Churches and graveyards are consecrated to provide protection, a good example of protection magic.

Boundary markers are a useful way to identify property lines. It's possible that these were originally used to protect the owner's property. The increasingly popular practice of smudging a room, house, or property is another form of protection magic.

In a sense you are performing magic any time you utilize some form of psychic protection. Wearing an amulet or gemstone for protection is an example.

Most people associate magic with the casting of spells. I cannot remember the first time I saw this being done, but it was probably when I was ten or eleven years old. I vividly recall watching new neighbors walking clockwise around their house three times while the wife held an egg in her raised hands. They finished by burying the egg in the front garden. I was dying to ask them what they were doing, but my parents wouldn't let me. I know now, of course, that they were conducting a ritual to protect their new home.

Traditionally, eggs have been used to absorb negative energy. Many years ago, I knew someone who regularly rubbed her body with a raw egg in the belief that it would absorb any negativity she had picked up during the day. When I lived in Cornwall, England, I met a lady who kept an egg on her bedside table. Every Saturday morning she would take the egg that had been sitting beside her for a week and bury it in her garden. She would then replace it with another one. Obviously, it is important to dispose of eggs that have absorbed negativity, and they should never be eaten. Although I have seen eggs being used to absorb negativity in a variety of ways, I have not used them myself for protection purposes.

You can use protection magic whenever you feel the need for it. A woman I met in southern France told me that she performed magic whenever she felt uneasy or anxious. The ritual she shared with me is simple, and can be adapted for any purpose.

Protection Magic Ritual

You will need some sacred, protected space to work within. Traditionally, this is a magic circle. You might like to construct a circle using cord or rope. Alternatively, you might like to mark out a circle using small objects, such as stones or crystals.[1] I have a large circular rug that works well. Another possibility is to imagine a circle.

Traditionally, magic circles are nine feet in diameter, and they were measured with a ceremonial cord that was four foot six inches long. However, it makes no difference if your magic circle is smaller or larger than this. If you live in a small home or apartment your magic circle may need to be considerably smaller than nine feet. Whenever possible, I perform my rituals outdoors. I live in a temperate climate and can work outdoors all year round, as long as it is not raining. In windy or wet weather I perform my rituals indoors.

You will need an altar to work on inside your circle. This can be a small table, or even part of a table, if nothing suitable is available. You will also need a small crystal, five white candles, a small bowl of water, and a dish of salt. If you wish to charge an object you intend using as a protective amulet, place it on your altar, too. Place one of the candles at the east side of your magic circle, one at the south, one at the west and one at the north. If space is limited you can arrange these candles in these positions on your altar. Place the fifth candle in a central position on your altar, with the bowls of water and salt in front of, and to each side of it. If you wish, you can add other items for aesthetic purposes. Additional candles, a bowl of freshly cut flowers, an attractive ornament, or photographs of the people you are intending to protect are good examples. Display these other objects on your altar in a semicircle behind the fifth candle.

Start by enjoying a leisurely bath or shower. You might like to add some salt to the bathwater to start the protection process before the ritual begins. While relaxing in the warm water, think about your intent in conducting the ritual, and what you intend to achieve as a result. When you get out of the bath, dry yourself vigorously with a clean towel, and dress yourself in clean, loose-fitting clothes.

Stand on the edge of your magic circle, close your eyes, and take three slow, deep breaths. Visualize yourself surrounded by a protective healing light. Open your eyes, and walk into the center of your circle. Face east and acknowledge the candle with a slight bow. Repeat with south, west, and north.

Light the candle in the east and hold it at chest height. Say: "I thank the element of air for blessing my sacred circle with friendship, love, and protection. Please protect me each and every day, no matter where I may go, or whatever I do." Replace the candle and turn to face south.

Light the candle in the south and hold it at chest height. Say: "I thank the element of fire for blessing my sacred circle with friendship, love, and protection. Please protect me each and every day, no matter where I may go, or whatever I do." Replace the candle and turn to face west.

Light the candle in the west and hold it at chest height. Say: "I thank the element of water for blessing my sacred circle with friendship, love, and protection. Please protect me each and every day, no matter where I may go, or whatever I do." Replace the candle and turn to face north.

Light the candle in the north and hold it at chest height. Say: "I thank the element of earth for blessing my sacred circle with friendship, love, and protection. Please protect me each and every day, no matter where I may go, or whatever I do." Replace the candle and light the candle on your altar.

Add three pinches of salt to the bowl of water, and spread your arms out wide. Slowly raise them upwards and visualize pure white light entering the fingers of each hand and spreading throughout your body. When you feel the white light has reached every cell of your body, say thank you out loud, and lower your arms.

Place the first finger of your dominant hand in the dish of water and say out loud:

Water and salt, protect me please
Keep me free from harm and all disease
Protect my home and loved ones, too
Protect my friends, both old and new
Avert any negativity aimed at me
An it harm none, so mote it be.

If you are using this ritual for general protection you can end it at this point by expressing your thanks to the four elements and extinguishing the candles. If you are requesting protection for a specific purpose, ask for it while your finger is still in the dish of water. The specific purpose can be anything that is concerning you.

An acquaintance of mine went through a terrible time when a man she had had a brief relationship with began stalking her. She performed this ritual every day until the man gave up and stopped following her.

If you are using this ritual to charge an amulet, you can, at this point, dip it into the water or, alternatively, sprinkle a few drops of water onto it.

Hold the amulet as high as you can for several seconds, and then tie it around your neck, or place it in a pocket. It is now ready to serve and protect you.

Remain at your altar for a few minutes, and think about the ritual you have just performed. When you feel ready, turn to the east and pick up the candle again. Hold it at chest height and say: "Thank you element of air for protecting me in every area of my life. My loved ones and I are truly grateful." Put the candle down and extinguish it using either your fingers or a candlesnuffer.

Repeat this process in the south, west, and north, thanking the elements of fire, water, and earth. Finally, return to your altar. Pick up the remaining candle and walk around the circumference of your magic circle. Place the candle back on the altar, and say: "I thank the powers of the universe for granting my request. This ritual is completed and the circle is closed. So mote it be."

Extinguish the candle using your fingers or a candlesnuffer and leave the circle. The ritual is over, but there is one final task to perform. Ground yourself by eating or drinking something. You might like to stamp your feet or go outside and touch the earth.

Wait at least ten minutes before picking up the container of salt water. Take it to the front door of your home and flick salted water all around the frame of the door. Sprinkle water around your windows, and around the outside walls of your house. If you have a garden, you can sprinkle water along all the boundary lines. Make sure to sprinkle some water on your mailbox, too.

Repeat this ritual whenever you feel anxious, worried, stressed out, or need protection. The words I have used in this ritual are my own. You can use my words if you wish, or create your own.

You can also embellish the ritual, if you wish. If you come from a Christian tradition, for instance, you might like to say a prayer at the start and finish of your rituals. If you have a Wiccan background you might like to use your athame (wand) to inscribe invoking pentagrams at each quarter, and follow that by drawing down the moon. A friend of mine has parents who are atheists, and grew up with no spiritual element in his life. He developed a ritual that was extremely matter-of-fact and clinical,

but it works well for him. After all, the most important aspect of this, or any other, ritual is the intent
behind it.

You can also visualize the entire ritual if you need
to perform it urgently for any reason. It is just as effective to do it this way, though visualizing the ritual
should be saved for emergencies, rather than as a re-
placement for physically performing it.

Banishing Knot Ritual

Knot magic is used for many purposes, including
warding off a psychic attack. If you know who is attacking you, you can "bind" the person by tying a
series of knots in a length of cord, and burying it in
the ground for three days. Once this time is up, you
can untie the knots and destroy the cord.

The knots are tied in specific positions along the
length of the cord. The cord can be any length, ranging from one to three yards. Mark one end to identify it, as you will have to untie the knots in the same
order you tied them.

As you tie the knots in the cord, think about the
person who is psychically attacking you. Tell yourself
that you will no longer accept any more of this person's evil thoughts or deeds, and by tying the knots
you are binding the person to prevent him or her
from attacking you again. Think of the outcome you
desire, and focus on this as you tighten each knot.

You will need to tie nine knots in the length of cord. Start by tying a knot at each end of the cord. The third knot is tied in the center. The fourth cord is tied midway between the knot at the left end of the cord and the center knot. The fifth knot is tied halfway between the knot at the right end and the one in the center. The sixth knot is tied halfway between the knot at the left end of the cord and the next knot. The seventh knot is tied halfway between the knot at the right end of the cord and the next knot. The eighth knot is tied halfway between the center knot and the next knot to its left. The ninth and final knot is tied halfway between the center knot and the closest knot to its right.

Once the knots have been tied, take the cord outside and bury it for three days. The person who is psychically attacking you is now powerless, as you have securely bound him or her with nine knots. You are now demonstrating what you think of this person's ill will by burying the cord for three days.

Dig up the cord at the same time of day that you buried it three days earlier. Untie each cord in the same order that you tied them in. As each knot becomes free, say out loud: "(Person's name), you have lost your power over me!" You might like to spit after saying these words to emphasize your complete and utter contempt of the person who attacked you. You should say these words with as much emphasis as you can, and increase your volume slightly with each one. As the final knot becomes undone, you should shout the words.

The cord now needs to be destroyed, as the power of the curse (the psychic attack) has been transferred into it. Make a small ritual out of burning the cord, and remember as you do so, that this is demonstrating that your magic is more powerful than that of the person attacking you.

Specific Person Candle Ritual

This ritual is performed only when you require protection from a specific person.

You will need seven colored candles to represent the colors of the rainbow and the chakras, a large white candle to represent you, and a small candle of whatever color you wish to represent the person you are seeking protection from.

Place the rainbow candles in a line across the back of your altar, with the red candle on your left when you face the altar, and the violet candle on your right. Place the white candle that represents you in the center of your altar. Place the final candle, on its side, immediately in front of your candle.

Light the seven candles of the rainbow, starting with the red one. Pause for a few moments after lighting it, and ask for protection for your root chakra. I like to visualize a ball of circling red energy in this part of my body. Repeat with the other six candles, each time asking for protection for the specific chakra, and visualizing the whirling energy in your body. Once you have done this, light the candle that represents you.

Sit down in front of your altar for a few minutes, gazing at the candles and visualizing yourself surrounded with divine white light. When you feel ready, pick up the candle that is lying on its side. This is the candle that represents the person from whom you are seeking protection.

Light this candle in the flame of the red candle. Look at it for several seconds, and then say: "The red in you has lost all its power." Blow the candle out, in the most contemptuous, dismissive way you can. Light the candle again, this time using the flame from the orange candle. As before, gaze at it for several seconds, and say: "The orange in you has lost all its power." Blow the candle out, in an even more contemptuous manner this time. Repeat with all the colors of the rainbow.

Once you have completed this, hold the candle in front of you and talk to it. After saying whatever you wish, finish by saying: "You have lost all your power over me. I am strong and divinely protected. You are weak, insignificant, and unimportant. You will never have any power over me, ever again."

You may like to finish the ritual by breaking this candle in half, and disposing of each half in a different place. If the person has affected you badly for a long period of time, you might like to repeat this ritual every day until his or her candle has been completely burned. Another useful way to dispose of the candle is to burn the remains outdoors under a full moon. This means the person ceases to exist as far as you are concerned, and he or she will be unable to affect you in any way.

How to Make a Witch Bottle

Witch bottles were a popular form of magical protection in the seventeenth and eighteenth centuries, especially in the United Kingdom. Archaeologists frequently find ancient witch bottles dating from this time. Witch bottles were usually made from heavy stoneware wine flagons known as bellarmine jugs, which came from the Rhineland. Cardinal Bellarmine (1542–1621) was a highly influential Catholic priest. The Protestants of his day tried to ridicule him by placing a caricature of his face on wine and beer jugs and bottles. Rather than undermining his influence, these bellarmines, as they were called, increased his reputation. When bellarmine jugs became unavailable in England, glass bottles were used instead.

An intact witch bottle dating from 1720 was found under a house in Reigate, England, in October 2000. When two professors from Loughborough University examined the contents, they found nine brass pins, pieces of clothing, animal and human hairs, an insect leg, a blade of grass, and human urine in it.[2]

A bottle with its cork studded with pins was found in the chimney of a farmhouse in Winterbourne Kingston, Dorset, in 1930. The bottle was full of liquid, possibly urine. Unfortunately, the bottle was accidentally broken and, as soon as that happened, the household lost their protection and experienced a run of bad luck.[3]

In 2004, the first totally intact witch bottle was found in Greenwich, South London. Before the bottle was opened, it was X-rayed and scanned, and some of the liquid was removed using a syringe through the cork. Tests conducted by Dr. Alan Massey, a retired lecturer from Loughborough University, revealed that the liquid was 300-year-old urine. The urine contained traces of nicotine, showing it came from a smoker. When the salt glaze bottle was opened, the scientists removed a small piece of leather in the shape of a heart, pierced by an iron nail, eight brass pins, a handful of bent iron nails, a lock of hair, ten nail clippings, traces of sulfur, and some navel lint. Dr. Massey examined the nail parings under a microscope and said, "From their size, they probably came from a male, and they were well manicured, so he was from a higher social class. It is possible that we could one day identify him from DNA analysis and the location of the discovery." Dr. Massey believes this witch bottle dates from between 1675 and 1700.[4]

A witch bottle is a glass or pottery container filled with sharp objects, such as pins, needles, nails, screws, and broken glass. Pieces of broken mirror are especially potent. The person making the bottle adds a small quantity of his or her urine and then seals the container before burying it. Sometimes, other items, such as saliva, stones, salt, and herbs are added to increase the protective qualities of the bottle. The bottle is usually buried close to the front door of the house, but it can be buried off the property, if desired.

Witch bottles provide protection and ward off any negativity. The witch bottle absorbs and neutralizes any negativity aimed at the home or the occupants.

Witch bottles are simple to make. The first step is to find a suitable container, such as a glass jar or bottle. One that is tinted amber or green is perfect, but a clear glass container will also work well. Collect a variety of sharp objects. Focus on your need for protection while placing the items into the container. Add some urine, and seal the container. If you don't want to use your own urine, you can substitute vinegar.

Make a small ceremony of burying the bottle. It should be buried close to the front door, in a place where it is unlikely to be disturbed. As you cover it with earth, thank it for providing you with protection. Your home will be protected as long as the bottle remains intact.

conclusion

It is natural to want to protect yourself, your loved ones, and your possessions. Fortunately, as you now know, you can do this in a variety of different ways.

However, it all begins inside your head. Your thoughts dictate your actions, and thinking positively about yourself is the first and most essential step in psychic protection.

The second most important step is to look after your aura, and make sure that it is kept strong at all times. Everyone is busy, and it's easy to neglect personal protection. However, as a strong aura plays such a vital role in every area of your life, it's well worth spending a few minutes every day looking after and nurturing your aura.

Be kind to yourself. We all make mistakes as we go through life. Everyone has regrets of one sort or another. Forgive yourself when you make a mistake. Learn from it, and move on.

Ensure you have some time for yourself every day. Allow enough time to relax and unwind. Meditate. Communicate with the divine. Eat healthy food, exercise, spend time with friends and family, laugh often, get enough sleep, and keep a sense of balance.

Base your life on positive principles such as forgiveness, honesty, love, loyalty, and responsibility. Develop faith, in yourself and in a higher power.

Expect good things to happen. Eventually, we all receive what we expect to receive. In reality, you are as lucky as you believe yourself to be. Expect good things to happen, and they will.

People need psychic protection most when they are feeling vulnerable. If you focus on remaining positive and concentrate on the good things in your life, you will be protected against most psychic attack. If you happen to experience a psychic attack of any sort, the material in this book will enable you to overcome it.

Now that you are fully armed and protected, I wish you great success and happiness.

notes

Introduction

1. Sheila Paine, *Amulets: A World of Secret Powers, Charms and Magic* (London: Thames & Hudson Limited, 2004), 11.

Chapter One

1. J. Maringer, *The Gods of Pre-Historic Man* (London: Weidenfeld & Nicolson Limited, 1960), 140, 170.

2. Carol Andrews, *Amulets of Ancient Egypt* (London: British Museum Press, 1994), 6–7.

3. G. and C. Charles-Picard, *Daily Life in Carthage* (London: Allen & Unwin Limited, 1961), 113.

4. E. A. Wallis Budge, *Amulets and Superstitions* (Oxford: Oxford University Press, 1930), xxvii.

5. C. J. S. Thompson, *Amulets, Talismans and Charms* (Edmonds, WA: Holmes Publishing Group, n.d.), 5–6.

6. Budge, 357–358.

7. R. Brasch, *The Supernatural and You!* (Stanmore, Australia: Cassell Australia Ltd., 1976), 142.

8. Ewa Wasilewska, *Creation Stories of the Middle East* (London: Jessica Kingsley Publishers, 2000), 137–138.

9. Richard Cavendish (editor), *Man, Myth and Magic*, vol. 2 (London: Purnell Books, 1970), 889.

10. Thomas and Katharine Macquoid, *About Yorkshire* (London: Chatto and Windus, 1883), 341.

11. William Carr, *The Dialect of Craven in the West Riding of the County of York*, vol. 1, 2nd ed. (London: William Crofts, 1828), 137.

12. Scott Cunningham and David Harrington, *The Magical Household* (St. Paul: Llewellyn Publications, 2002), 58.

13. *Encyclopaedia Britannica Micropaedia*, vol. 3, 15th ed. (Chicago, IL: Encyclopaedia Britannica, Inc., 1974), 1017.

14. Frederick Thomas Elworthy, *The Evil Eye* (London: John Murray and Company, 1895), 204. Reprinted by Dover Publications, 2004.

15. T. Schrire, *Hebrew Amulets: Their Decipherment and Interpretation* (London: Routledge & Kegan Paul Ltd., 1966), 7.

16. Rosemary Ellen Guiley, *The Encyclopedia of Witches and Witchcraft* (New York: Facts On File, Inc., 1989), 135.

Chapter Two

1. Robin Skelton, *The Magical Practice of Talismans* (Victoria, British Columbia: Beach Holme Publishers, 1991), 16.

2. Andrew D. White, *History of the Warfare of Science with Theology* (1897, reprinted Chicago: Chicago University Press, 1997), 343.

3. Budge, 315.

4. Nigel Pennick, *The Secret Lore of Runes and Other Ancient Alphabets* (London: Rider and Company, 1991), 204.

5. Harvey Day, *Occult Illustrated Dictionary* (London: Kaye and Ward, 1975), 129.

6. Richard Webster, *Amulets and Talismans for Beginners* (St. Paul: Llewellyn Publications, 2004), 103–113. This book contains several different methods for charging a talisman.

Chapter Three

1. Michael Howard, *Incense and Candle Burning,* rev. ed. (London: Aquarian Press, 1991), 97.

2. Eric Maple, *Man, Myth and Magic,* ed. Richard Cavendish (London: Purnell Books, 1970), 2167.

3. O. Alaoui-Ismaielie et al., "Basic Emotions Evoked by Odorants." *Physiology and Behavior* 62 (1997), 713.

4. In reference to perfumes, "amber" is not made from fossilized tree resins; it is almost impossible to extract oil from these ancient gems. Perfumeries create fragrance combinations that call to mind amber's appearance in scent: warm, earthy, sensuous, and honey-like fragrances.

5. Exodus 30:27–38, 37:29; Leviticus 2:1–16, 6:15, 10:1, 16:13, 24:7–9; Numbers 16:46–47; Luke 1:9–11; and Revelation 8:3–4.

6. Plutarch, quoted in *Berossos and Manetho*, introduced and translated by Gerald P. Verbrugghe and John M. Wickersham (Ann Arbor, MI: University of Michigan Press, 2001), 166.

7. Carl Neal, *Incense: Crafting and Use of Magickal Scents* (St. Paul: Llewellyn Publications, 2003); Scott Cunningham, *The Complete Book of Incense, Oils and Brews* (St. Paul: Llewellyn Publications, 1989); Steven R. Smith, *Wylundt's Book of Incense* (York Beach: Samuel Weiser, Inc., 1989); Susanne Fischer-Rizzi, *The Complete Incense Book* (New York: Sterling Publications, 1988); Leo Vinci, *Incense: Its Ritual Significance, Use and Preparation* (London: Aquarian Press, 1980).

Chapter Four

1. Michael Weinstein, *The World of Jewel Stones* (London: Sir Isaac Pitman and Son, 1959), 3.

2. George Frederick Kunz, *The Curious Lore of Precious Stones* (Philadelphia: J. B. Lippincott Company, 1913), 35–37. The larger necklace contained three carnelian pendants of the god Bes, seven carnelian pendants of the goddess Toeris (plus two in lapis lazuli), a heart shape of lapis lazuli, four falcons of carnelian, one crocodile of carnelian and two

of lapis lazuli, four fish of carnelian, one fish of a blackish white stone, one fish of a green stone, two scorpions of carnelian, and seven flower shapes of carnelian.

3. George Frederick Kunz, *The Curious Lore of Precious Stones*, 38–39.

4. Ibid., 24.

5. Ibid., 307.

6. Bruce G. Knuth, *Gems in Myth, Legend and Lore* (Thornton: Jewelers Press, 1999), 236.

7. Aleister Crowley, *777 and Other Qabalistic Writings of Aleister Crowley* (Boston: Samuel Weiser, Inc., 1977). (Originally published anonymously in 1909.)

8. Harriet Keith Fobes, *Mystic Gems* (Boston: Richard G. Badger, 1924), 58–59.

9. Sir Jean de Mandeville's Lapidary was first printed in France in 1520 as *Le lapidaire en francoys, compose par Messire Jehan de Mandeville, chevalier.* However, there is some doubt as to its authorship, as it is not included in any editions of his collected works. Regardless of who wrote it, this was the first popular lapidary to be published, and it was extremely successful.

10. Marguerite Elsbeth, *Crystal Medicine* (St. Paul: Llewellyn Publications, 1997), 166.

11. S. O. Addy, *Household Tales, with Other Traditional Remains Collected in the Counties of York, Lincoln, Derby and Nottingham* (London: David Nutt in the Strand, 1895), xiv.

Chapter Five

1. Carole Potter, *Knock on Wood and Other Superstitions* (New York: Sammis Publishing, 1983), 112.

2. George Frederick Kunz, *The Magic of Jewels and Charms* (Philadelphia: J. B. Lippincott Company, 1915), 337–338.

Chapter Eight

1. Margaret Baker, *Folklore and Customs of Rural England* (Newton Abbot: David & Charles [Holdings] Limited, 1974), 135.

2. Although Lilith was first mentioned in the *Alphabet of Ben Sira*, it is possible that she was one of the female demons in Babylonian mythology known as *Lilitu*.

3. E. A. Wallis Budge, *Amulets and Superstitions* (London: Oxford University Press, 1930), 224. Two illustrations of amulets used to protect mothers and their babies from the *Book of Raziel* are shown on pages 225 and 226.

4. C. J. S. Thompson, *Hand of Destiny* (London: Rider & Company, Limited, 1932), 116–117.

5. R. Brasch, *How Did it Begin?* (London: Longman, Green & Co. Ltd., 1965), 22–23.

Chapter Nine

1. Richard Cavendish (editor), *Man, Myth and Magic*, Vol 6 (London: Purnell Books, 1971), 2613. Also, C. J. S. Thompson, *The Hand of Destiny* (London: Rider & Company Limited, 1932), 83–84.

2. Richard Webster, *The Encyclopedia of Superstitions* (Woodbury: Llewellyn Publications, 2008), 126.

3. Richard Webster, *101 Feng Shui Tips for the Home* (St. Paul: Llewellyn Publications, 1998), 79–91.

Chapter Ten

1. B. B. Wiffen, *Choice Notes from 'Notes and Queries': Folk Lore* (London: Bell and Daldy, 1859), 129–130.

2. Juliette de Bairacli-Levy, *Wanderers in the New Forest* (London: Faber & Faber Limited, 1958), 125–126.

3. Margaret Baker, *Folklore and Customs of Rural England* (Newton Abbot: David & Charles Holdings Ltd., 1974), 59.

4. Margaret Baker, *Folklore and Customs of Rural England*, 62.

5. C. J. S. Thompson, *The Hand of Destiny* (London: Rider and Company Ltd., 1932), 141.

6. E. & M. A. Radford, edited and revised by Christina Hole, *Encyclopaedia of Superstitions* (London: Hutchinson & Co. [Publishers] Ltd., 1961), 204.

7. Stephen Pollington, *Leechcraft: Early English Charms, Plantlore and Healing* (Hockwold-cum-Wilton, UK: Anglo-Saxon Books, 2000), 71.

8. Pseudo-Apuleius, quoted in Lesley Gordon, *The Mystery and Magic of Trees and Flowers* (London: Webb & Bower [Publishers] Limited, 1985), 58.

9. William Coles, *The Art of Simpling* (London, 1656. Reprinted by Pomeroy: Health Research, n.d.), 87.

10. Machaelle Small Wright, *Perelandra Garden Workbook: A Complete Guide to Gardening with Nature Intelligences* (Jeffersonton: Perelandra, Ltd., 1987).

11. Reader's Digest, *Magic and Medicine of Plants* (The Reader's Digest Association, Inc., 1994), 10.

Chapter Eleven

1. Leonard George, *Alternative Realities: The Paranormal, the Mystic and the Transcendent in Human Experience* (New York: Facts on File, Inc., 1995), 170–171.

Chapter Twelve

1. Eileen Edna Power, *Medieval English Nunneries, c. 1275–1535* (Cheshire, CT: Biblo and Tannen, 1988), 677.

2. Malcolm Barber, *The Trial of the Templars* (Cambridge, UK: Cambridge University Press, 1978), 285.

3. C. J. S. Thompson, *The Hand of Destiny* (London: Rider and Company, 1932), 163–164.

4. Dion Fortune, *Psychic Self-Defence: A Study in Occult Pathology and Criminality* (London: Rider & Company Limited, 1930. Republished by Samuel Weiser, Inc., 1957), 152.

5. Dion Fortune, *Ceremonial Magic Unveiled*. Article in *Occult Review*, January 1933.

Chapter Thirteen

1. You can use any gemstones or crystal you wish to mark out your magic circle. The following stones are the ones that are traditionally associated with the four cardinal directions: EAST citrine, topaz SOUTH amber,

garnet, obsidian, ruby WEST aquamarine, chalcedony, jade, lapis lazuli, moonstone NORTH moss agate, emerald, jet, black tourmaline.

2. Ray Buckland, *The Witch Book: The Encyclopedia of Witchraft, Wicca, and Neo-Paganism* (Detroit: Visible Ink Press, 2002), 525.

3. Marianne R. Dacombe (editor), *Dorset Up Along and Down Along* (Dorchester: Dorset Federation of Women's Institutes, 1935), 116.

4. Simon de Bruxelles, "Witch Bottle is Uncorked to Discover Spellbinding Content." *The Times* online. http://www.timesonline. co.uk/tol/news/uk/science/article6426318 .ece?print=yes&randnu... (accessed June 4, 2009).

suggested reading

Andrews, Carol. *Amulets of Ancient Egypt*. London: British Museum Press, 1994.

Andrews, Ted. *Psychic Protection*. Jackson, TN: Dragonhawk Publishing, 1998.

Baker, Margaret. *Folklore and Customs of Rural England*. Newton Abbot, UK: David & Charles (Holdings) Limited, 1974.

Crowson, Michael. *Psychic Lifeline: A Quick Guide to Recognizing and Managing Psychic or Occult Harm*. Brighton, UK: Omnigen, 2006.

Cuhulain, Kerr. *Magickal Self Defense: A Quantum Approach to Warding*. Woodbury, MN: Llewellyn Publications, 2008.

Cunningham, Scott. *The Complete Book of Incense, Oils and Brews*. St. Paul, MN: Llewellyn Publications, 1989.

Evans, Joan. *Magical Jewels of the Middle Ages and the Renaissance*. Oxford: Oxford University Press, 1922.

Fortune, Dion. *Psychic Self-Defence: A Study in Occult Pathology and Criminality*. New York: Samuel Weiser, Inc., 1957. (First published 1930.)

Gordon, Lesley. *The Mystery and Magic of Trees and Flowers*. London: Webb & Bower (Publishers) Limited, 1985.

Hall, Judy. *Way of Psychic Protection*. London: Thorsons, 2001.

Hall, Judy. *The Art of Psychic Protection*. San Francisco: Red Wheel/Weiser, 1997.

Hazlitt, W. C. *Dictionary of Faiths and Folklore*. London: Reeves and Turner, 1905.

John-Roger. *Psychic Protection*. Los Angeles: Mendeville Press, 1976. Revised edition, 1997.

Kunz, George Frederick. *The Curious Lore of Precious Stones*. Philadelphia: J. B. Lippincott Company, 1913.

Kunz, George Frederick. *The Magic of Jewels and Charms*. Philadelphia: J. B. Lippincott Company, 1915.

Mason, Henry M. *The Seven Secrets of Crystal Talismans*. Woodbury, MN: Llewellyn Publications, 2008.

Mickaharic, Draja. *Spiritual Cleansing: A Handbook of Psychic Protection*. York Beach, ME: Weiser Books, 1982.

Miller, Jason. *Protection & Reversal Magick: A Witch's Defense Manual*. Franklin Lakes, NJ: New Page Books, 2006.

Paine, Sheila. *Amulets: A World of Secret Powers, Charms and Magic*. London: Thames & Hudson Limited, 2004.

Penczak, Christopher. *The Witch's Shield: Protection Magick & Psychic Self-Defence*. St. Paul, MN: Llewellyn Publications, 2004.

Pollington, Stephen. *Leechcraft: Early English Charms, Plantore and Healing*. Hockwold-cum-Wilton, UK: Anglo-Saxon Books, 2000.

Radford, E. & M. A. *Encyclopaedia of Superstitions*. London: Hutchinson & Co. (Publishers) Limited, 1948. New edition, edited and revised by Christina Hole, 1961.

Thompson, C. J. S. *The Hand of Destiny*. London: Rider & Company, 1932. Reprinted by Kessinger Publishing, n.d.

Webster, Richard. *Flower and Tree Magic: Discover the Natural Enchantment Around You*. Woodbury, MN: Llewellyn Publications, 2008.

———. *The Encyclopedia of Superstitions*. Woodbury, MN: Llewellyn Publications, 2008.

———. *Amulets and Talismans for Beginners*. St. Paul, MN: Llewellyn Publications, 2004.

———. *Candle Magic for Beginners*. St. Paul, MN: Llewellyn Publications, 2004.

———. *Pendulum Magic for Beginners*. St. Paul, MN: Llewellyn Publications, 2002.

———. *Aura Reading for Beginners*. St. Paul, MN: Llewellyn Publications, 1998.

———. *101 Feng Shui Tips for the Home*. St. Paul, MN: Llewellyn Publications, 1998.

Wright, Machaelle Small. *Perelandra Garden Workbook: A Complete Guide to Gardening with Nature Intelligences*. Jeffersonton, VA: Perelandra, Ltd., 1987.

index

GET MORE AT LLEWELLYN.COM

Visit us online to browse hundreds of our books and decks, plus sign up to receive our e-newsletters and exclusive online offers.

- • Free tarot readings • Spell-a-Day • Moon phases
- • Recipes, spells, and tips • Blogs • Encyclopedia
- • Author interviews, articles, and upcoming events

GET SOCIAL WITH LLEWELLYN

Find us on
Facebook
www.Facebook.com/LlewellynBooks

Follow us on

www.Twitter.com/Llewellynbooks

GET BOOKS AT LLEWELLYN

LLEWELLYN ORDERING INFORMATION

Order online: Visit our website at www.llewellyn.com to select your books and place an order on our secure server.

Order by phone:
- • Call toll free within the U.S. at 1-877-NEW-WRLD (1-877-639-9753)
- • Call toll free within Canada at 1-866-NEW-WRLD (1-866-639-9753)
- • We accept VISA, MasterCard, and American Express

Order by mail:
Send the full price of your order (MN residents add 6.875% sales tax) in U.S. funds, plus postage and handling to: Llewellyn Worldwide, 2143 Wooddale Drive Woodbury, MN 55125-2989

POSTAGE AND HANDLING:

STANDARD: (U.S., Mexico & Canada)
(Please allow 2 business days)
$25.00 and under, add $4.00.
$25.01 and over, FREE SHIPPING.

INTERNATIONAL ORDERS (airmail only):
$16.00 for one book, plus $3.00 for each additional book.

Visit us online for more shipping options. Prices subject to change.

FREE CATALOG!

To order, call
1-877-
NEW-WRLD
ext. 8236
or visit our
website

CANDLE MAGIC FOR BEGINNERS
The Simplest Magic You Can Do
RICHARD WEBSTER

Anyone who has made a wish before blowing out birthday candles has practiced candle magic. Quick, easy, and effective, this magical art requires no religious doctrine or previous magic experience. Anyone can practice candle magic and Richard Webster shows you how to get started. Learn how to perform rituals, spells, and divinations to gain luck, love, prosperity, protection, healing, and happiness. Also included are tips for which kinds of candles to use, candle maintenance and preparation, best times for magic, and how to make your own candles.

978-0-7387-0535-4
264 pp., 5³⁄₁₆ x 8 $13.95

Spanish edition:
Velas mágicas para principiantes
978-0-7387-0647-4 $12.95

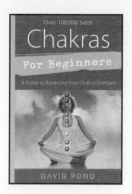

CHAKRAS FOR BEGINNERS
A Guide to Balancing Your Chakra Energies
DAVID POND

The chakras are spinning vortexes of energy located just in front of your spine and positioned from the tailbone to the crown of the head. They are a map of your inner world—your relationship to yourself and how you experience energy. They are also the batteries for the various levels of your life energy. The freedom with which energy can flow back and forth between you and the universe correlates directly to your total health and well-being.

The chakras stand out as the most useful model for you to identify how your energy is expressing itself. With *Chakras for Beginners* you will discover what is causing any imbalances, how to bring your energies back into alignment, and how to achieve higher levels of consciousness.

978-1-56718-537-9
192 pp., 5³⁄₁₆ x 8 $11.95

Spanish edition:
Chakras para principiantes
978-1-56718-536-2

CRYSTALS FOR BEGINNERS
A Guide to Collecting & Using Stones & Crystals
CORRINE KENNER

Revered for their beauty, unique electrical qualities, and metaphysical attributes, crystals have been precious to mankind for centuries. *Crystals for Beginners* explores the universal allure of crystals and demonstrates how to channel their dynamic energies.

Beginning with how crystals were formed in the Earth billions of years ago, this practical guide introduces the history and myth surrounding these powerful minerals. From agates to zoisite, the characteristics of specific crystals are presented, along with advice for collecting, cleansing, and charging them. Readers also learn how to apply crystal energy to meditation, healing, psychic development, magic, divination, astral projection, dream work, and much more.

978-0-7387-0755-6
264 pp., 5³⁄₁₆ x 8 $13.95

JEWELRY & GEMS FOR SELF-DISCOVERY
Choosing Gemstones That Delight the Eye and Strengthen the Soul
SHAKTI CAROLA NAVRAN

Have you ever fallen in love with a ring or necklace? Perhaps there's a reason! Gems and crystals have metaphysical and healing qualities that can support you physically, emotionally, and spiritually. This innovative guide will help you choose a piece of jewelry ideal for your unique life path.

Diamonds enhance your creativity. Rubies teach us about love. Opals fuel intuition and offer healing. Which stones are right for you? Shakti Carola Navran offers a thorough introduction to astrology to help you identify the challenges and spiritual needs evident in your birth chart. A detailed list of sixty-four gems and crystals—with full-color photos of polished stones and finished jewelry—makes it easy to find the minerals that can balance these conflicting energies. You'll learn how to "program" your stone with joy, peace of mind, self-confidence, or any other quality. There's also helpful information for choosing the form (ring, earrings, or necklace), selecting the metal setting, and incorporating symbols into your unique piece of jewelry.

978-0-7387-1443-1

216 pp., 6 x 9 $16.95

16-page full-color photo insert of gems, stones, and finished jewelry

---

INSTANT MAGICK
Ancient Wisdom, Modern Spellcraft
CHRISTOPHER PENCZAK

What if you could practice magick anytime, without the use of ceremonial spells, altars, or magickal tools? Items such as candles, special ingredients, and exotic symbols are necessary to perform many types of magick, but these items aren't always feasible, attainable, or even available. The purest form of magick—tapping into your own energetic awareness to create change—is accessible simply through the power of your will.

Popular author Christopher Penczak explains how to weave natural energies into every facet of life by inspiring readers to explore their own individual willpower. This book features personalized techniques used to weed out any unwanted, unhealthy, or unnecessary desires to find a true, balanced magickal being. Penczak's innovative, modern spellcasting techniques utilize meditation, visualization, words, and intent in any situation, at any time. The results can seem instantaneous, and the potential limitless.

978-0-7387-0859-1
216 pp., 6 x 9 $13.95

Magickal Self Defense
A Quantum Approach to Warding
Kerr Cuhulain

As a Wiccan who spent twenty-eight years on the police force, Kerr Cuhulain knows a thing or two about self-defense. The author of *Wiccan Warrior* and *Full Contact Magick* returns with a powerful program for magickal protection—based on the principles of the Witches' Pyramid, chi energy, and quantum science.

From everyday stress to the emotions of people around you, negative energy is everywhere. This innovative guide not only advises on how to cope with negative energies, but it also offers a fascinating explanation of how magick works in our quantum universe. Beginning and advanced magical practitioners will learn how to safely thwart psychic attacks, develop threat awareness, balance chi, create an astral temple for refuge, and use magickal tools for defense. Cuhulain also evaluates traditional methods of self-defense—energy traps, mirroring, fire, fumigation, sigils—and debunks many protection myths.

978-0-7387-1219-2
240 pp., 6 x 9 $15.95

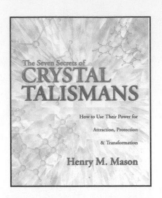

THE SEVEN SECRETS OF CRYSTAL TALISMANS
How to Use Their Power for Attraction, Protection & Transformation
HENRY M. MASON

The mysterious powers of gems, crystals, and minerals are finally explained in this practical guide to creating talismans. Casting a modern light on the age-old practice of talismans, gemologist Henry M. Mason correlates the mystical properties of these wondrous objects with the science of gemology.

Connecting with the universal life force, the proper talisman can focus and magnify your own qualities—helping you fulfill dreams and desires. Mason's seven secrets explore how crystal structure, color, and chemistry contribute to a talisman's natural energies for aiding in attraction, protection, self-improvement, creativity, tranquility, spiritual awakening, and more. From selecting and preparing the proper mineral to empowering your talisman, this guide takes you through every step of creating and using talismans and amulets for optimum effect.

978-0-7387-1144-7
240 pp., 7½ x 9⅛ $17.95
28-page full-color insert

TO ORDER, CALL 1-877-NEW-WRLD
Prices subject to change without notice
Order at Llewellyn.com 24 hours a day, 7 days a week!

FENG SHUI IN FIVE MINUTES
SELENA SUMMERS

The world's most easy-to-use guide to feng shui!

To prosper, is it better to live in a small house in a wealthy area or a large house in a less expensive area? How can a radio, television set, or computer be a feng shui cure? What are the luckiest shapes for blocks of land?

These are just three of the many questions you'll find answered in *Feng Shui in Five Minutes*. Learn intriguing no-cost methods to improve your luck, a mystic way to hurry house sales, ancient techniques to win more dates, the Nine Celestial Cures, common feng shui faults, and much more.

978-0-7387-0291-9
216 pp., 5³⁄₁₆ x 8   **$12.95**

THE COMPLETE BOOK OF INCENSE, OILS & BREWS
SCOTT CUNNINGHAM

For centuries the composition of incenses, the blending of oils, and the mixing of herbs have been used by people to create positive changes in their lives. With this book, the curtains of secrecy have been drawn back, providing you with practical, easy-to-understand information that will allow you to practice these methods of magical cookery.

There is no special, costly equipment to buy, and ingredients are usually easy to find. The book includes detailed information on a wide variety of herbs, sources for purchasing ingredients, substitutions for hard-to-find herbs, a glossary, and a chapter on creating your own magical recipes.

978-0-87542-128-5
288 pp., 6 x 9   **$16.95**

Spanish edition:
Inciensos, Aceites, e Infusiones
304 pp., 5³⁄₁₆ x 8½ $11.95